T0064108

A Sliver of Sky

A Sliver of Sky

KYRA RAI

PARTRIDGE
A Penguin Random House Company

Copyright © 2015 by Kyra Rai.

ISBN:	Hardcover	978-1-4828-4774-1
	Softcover	978-1-4828-4773-4
	eBook	978-1-4828-4772-7

All rights reserved. No part of this book may be used or reproduced by any means, graphic, electronic, or mechanical, including photocopying, recording, taping or by any information storage retrieval system without the written permission of the publisher except in the case of brief quotations embodied in critical articles and reviews.

Because of the dynamic nature of the Internet, any web addresses or links contained in this book may have changed since publication and may no longer be valid. The views expressed in this work are solely those of the author and do not necessarily reflect the views of the publisher, and the publisher hereby disclaims any responsibility for them.

This is a work of fiction. Names, characters, businesses, places, events and incidents are either the products of the author's imagination or used in a fictitious manner. Any resemblance to actual persons, living or dead, or actual events is purely coincidental.

Print information available on the last page.

To order additional copies of this book, contact
Partridge India
000 800 10062 62
orders.india@partridgepublishing.com

www.partridgepublishing.com/india

Contents

A Sliver of Sky

Ten year old Rekha tentatively tugged at the old woman's sari to see if it evoked any reaction. The old woman turned from the window and smiled gently at her. 'Why are you always standing near that window? What are you looking for?' Rekha asked the woman.

'I am not looking *for* something, child, I am looking *at* my life that is past.' Sighing loudly she sank down to the floor, resting her back against the wall. She glanced at the people in the fairly large room. They were mostly women around her age with a few girls aged between 9 – 12 years. Some of the women were staring vacantly into space while the children engaged themselves playing with each other. The women were dressed uniformly in light blue saris and the girls in similar colored ankle length skirts with matching blouses. Each had a mat, pillow and bedsheet to spread out for sleeping. In one corner of the room was a washbasin into which the murky water from half closed tap was leaking.

Usha had never thought that she would end up spending the last days of her life in a destitute home. Maybe ten years back she would have raved that she would rather end her life. But, she realized that one's birth and death are pre ordained and she had no role in her life except live it.

'What was your life that is past like?' Rekha asked. 'Have you lived in this place since you were as old as me?'

'No, child, it is only one year since I came here, I lived in that world outside the window for so many years… so much has happened and it is all over…my role in life is over,' the woman replied.

'Tell me about that life…' Rekha asked. Running her fingers gently through Rekha's hair, she started her story. Slowly the other women in the Home gathered round to hear Ushamma's story.

I was born on September 19 1945, in a hospital near Brickhousepeta, Nellore, Andhra Pradesh. Ammama[1], my maternal grandmother was living there on my grandfather's ancestral property after she walked out on him following his second marriage in Hyderabad. Since it was customary for women to go to their natal homes for childbirth, my mother came to my grandmother's home in Nellore for my birth also. It was the time of the Telengana Armed Peasant Struggle. The Communist Party was part of the struggle. My father, great uncles, paternal and maternal uncles were very much involved in it. It seems that when my father came to see me all he said was that he was happy that I was normal.

I was a chubby nine pound rosy pink, healthy baby and everyone rejoiced at my birth though I was the fourth child. My mother quite often used to tell me, in most uncomplimentary terms whenever she wanted to express her displeasure at something I had done, that when she had to whisper a name in my ear at my cradling ceremony, she whispered 'Usha…my gentle rosy dawn' Of course the belief, then as now was that, just like the early morning sun I would be gentle, soft and warm as an ideal woman should be; and what a horrid creature I turned out to be!

---

[1]   Ammama – mother's mother

My birth is recorded as given above. The rest is narrative that I gleaned from various conversations. I don't remember ever having sat down and asked about my birth or reasons for naming me what they had named me. I am a curiously incurious creature. I hardly ever ask questions. I have always felt that it is not proper on the part of any human being to probe another's life by asking personal questions. While the questions I would ask pertained to my birth, they would also transgress on the right of my parents and relatives to name me as they pleased. If I did not like the name I had the option of dropping it either by requesting that people do not call me by that name or by totally changing it legally at any point of time after attaining adulthood!

In retrospect, I can only conclude that both my conservative Tamil Brahmin parents in their own way, saw in me something different – the makings of a leader, a gentle but firm mother lighting the path for the millions groping in the dark! This is just a conjecture that pleases me because from what I have got to know of my parents over many years, I doubt if they consciously thought of me as being blessed with any such qualities!

By the time I was 18 months old I fell sick and this sickness continued till I was seven years old. My parents and grandparents used to recall how I was on my mother's lap for seven years continuously. This must be exaggeration but it sounds very romantic and I have never failed to recount it to willing listeners! There was no clear diagnosis as to what my illness was and my parents ran from one doctor to another, kept trying all streams of medicine to cure me but they were told that there was no hope of my survival and it was a question of time before I breathed my last. As I grew older and started consulting doctors for my various illnesses I tried explaining this childhood health condition and it was always heard with an air of bored skepticism. After some years I simply dropped the whole episode from my medical history.

Ours was a lower middle class Brahmin family. I was told that on my father's side, my great grandfather migrated to Hyderabad in search of work and in those days Hyderabad was part of Madras Presidency. Thatha,[2] my paternal grandfather only completed his high school due to financial constraints but was a wizard with numbers. He had solved all the problems in Professor Sambamurthi's[3] Arithmetic book but he could not publish this key to the arithmetic book due to lack of money. My paternal grandmother (Appamma[4] to me) was just 9 years old when she got married. Thatha started working as a clerk in the British Railways and educated his two younger brothers and also his three sons. He had one daughter who died as a child. I heard that Appamma was deeply affected by the death of this only daughter. I remember that as long as Appamma was alive, she used to always donate a set of clothes to a girl once a year in memory of that daughter. And since I was anyway a child in the house I used to be given this set of clothes sometimes. When she was in a very affectionate mood she would call me 'Chemmini' (the name of her daughter).

Appamma was an extremely beautiful woman. Tall and well built, she was fair skinned, with large expressive eyes and naturally well shaped eyebrows. Even at the age of 60, she had thick long hair which fell below her knees. Her eyes sparkled as if in competition with the diamond studs adorning her ears and nose. Till she fell very sick with cancer, she would always

---

2   Thatha - grandfather

3   Professor Sambamurthi – a renowned mathematician who had designed the high school text books in the 19th century

4   Appama – Father's mother

be clad in a Kancheepuram silk sari, hair tied in a neat bun at the nape of her neck and wore long strands of pearls, corals and gold falling down the neck to her ample bosom. She used a walking stick due to being afflicted by rheumatism but she was very active. Without sounding snobbish I must say that both my maternal and paternal families were exceedingly good looking!

My maternal grandmother, Ammama[5], was also around 9 when she was married off to a medical doctor. Being a medical doctor in those days was akin to being God and Vasuthatha seemed to have enjoyed the advantages of that. They had three sons and two daughters. Just after my mother who was second in the line of children and a mere 13 years old was married off, it seems that Vasuthatha brought home a widow and told Ammama that he had married her and she would also live in the same house. I marvel at Ammama's courage given the time in which she lived, her limited options and heavy liabilities. It seems she simply refused and opted to take her dependent children and go and live in Nellore in the ancestral home of Vasuthata. There was a piece of agricultural land and Vasuthatha's younger brother lived in one portion of the house with his family. She had three sons to educate and one daughter to marry off. She was so young herself. Her eldest son (Perimama) took off and joined the army and then the Communist Party. They had barely enough to eat, leave alone her educating the children. As she narrated in her meanderings many years later, it was not an easy life because the fact that she was single meant that she had to carefully fend off sexual advances from her brother-in-law. Somehow she managed to educate my two uncles Seshumama and Rajamama and also aunt Jayamma. Then Ammama's elder sister who lived

---

[5] Ammama – maternal grandmother

in Madras[6] took them over and with an understanding that some quantity of the rice crop would be sent to her she moved with the children to Madras. My parents' marriage also was a case of child marriage – Appa was 17 years and Amma was 13 years. My sister, Asha, was born when Amma was 15 years old.

One of the traditions that I hated was that for the summer vacations we always had to go to Madras. Ammama was there with my two uncles – Seshumama and Rajamama. They all loved me and pampered me to whatever extent was possible given the limited resources they had. Unfortunately, humid weather does not suit me to date and I always fell sick during such visits with ailments that traumatized me and my family. I remember waking up one morning during a vacation in Madras, with itching and burning on my back and chest. As the day progressed, the small spots turned into huge boils with gaping pus spots. The doctor was called and he said it was an attack of herpes. There was no cure for it and the only way the burning could be reduced was by painting around the boils with something like brick paste. The smell of this paste was in itself cooling and satisfying as long as the wetness lasted. For maybe a half hour there would be relief and I would again start screaming. I wanted to go back to Hyderabad immediately. Ammama explained that the boils had to subside before we could travel and so I bore the pain and discomfort as best I could. Both my grandmothers always wondered at the patience with which I bore the pain of my illness from such a young age.

When my parents or my paternal uncle Srinu used to narrate some of the episodes of my illness it amused me greatly. At the same time it also fills me with happiness and gratitude

---

[6]   Madras – now known as Chennai

that I was blessed with such a caring family. It seems that during the time when I was sick with nephritis, if I was shifted even slightly I would scream nonstop. Similarly, I was told, that if I was denied something I wanted I would start screaming. Since I could hardly articulate words clearly due to my illness, my family would spend hours together trying to figure out the reason for my screaming and what it was that I wanted or that disturbed me. They tried every kind of cure under the sun for me – feeding me donkey's milk, goat's milk, steamed fish. Someone said that black magic would help and they tried that treatment also. During this illness of seven years it seems that I stubbornly got my head shaved seven times because I could not tolerate the prickliness of my thick hair. After running from pillar to post to find some cure for my illness, my parents were guided to a doctor called Dr. Borgaonker. He too did not succeed in arriving at a diagnosis and then recommended we try a homeopath in Hyderabad. It was finally this homeopath, Dr. Chinnana, who diagnosed my illness and cured me. This miracle man, Dr. Chinnana was my doctor till he became too infirm to attend to any patients and finally died. I eventually got cured of what some doctors called acute nephritis and some others called some kind of intestinal condition. Hardly had I recovered than I contracted typhoid. Dr. Chinnana it seems said that it was good I contracted typhoid since it was an indication of my body getting back to normal. By this time I was almost eight years old and can still remember the feeling of tremendous fatigue during this illness. As a result of the number of head shaves I had, my hair grew really thick, curly and long. I was admitted into St. Hilda School when I was 8 years old. Even through the period of my illness, during the brief days of respite from physical suffering that I enjoyed, Thatha used to teach me the English alphabet, numbers and simple arithmetic and nursery rhymes. It seems I was a quick learner with a curious mind. So by the time I got into school, I was ready to get into Class 1. All the children would be grouped into sections – A to D according to their academic excellence so I was always in A Section throughout my schooling. In fact, I was one of those rare students who got a double promotion – from Class 1 to Class 3. I was very thin and fragile physically but a voracious reader. My lack of participation in sports was made up by the speed with which I read books. Thatha encouraged this by buying me books of various authors.

During the 'games' period I would always sit it out in the shade of a tree skirting the sports field while my classmates ran around screaming and shouting with frenzy and excitement. All of them would try to stop by midway and pat me on the head, with understanding and compassion. In the beginning I used to feel left out and particularly humiliated when the sports teacher unfailingly made fun of me, before she got the rest of the girls on the field. I always wondered why she behaved in such a manner and why she never let go of a chance to rile me. I think something happens to us when we grow up into adults – we become hurtful and rude for no reason.

In school we used to have two badges awarded every month – one read 'First in Class' and the other read 'Good Conduct.' I most often got both the badges every month. If not I was a close second. In Class 3 I was made Class Monitor and so had to forego the race for 'Good Conduct' because only one whose conduct was impeccable could become monitor! The student who stood first in class for the maximum number of times was awarded a gold medal at the Annual Day. This eluded me throughout because I would always fall sick at least twice or more times in a year and so forfeit my 'rightful' place for that, many times. This was something that bothered me greatly for several years after I finished school.

Though not a mischievous child, I always had a mind of my own and was a self-affirmed 'loyalist.' To illustrate: the primary school students had morning assembly in the open and Ms. Phillips used to preside, where we all had to stand at attention, hands folded and repeat the prayer after her. I think she would open her eyes for a sweeping glance at us every now and then. It so happened that one boy who was standing next to me was pushed by the boy next to him and staggered against me which made me move and shuffle and open my eyes. She caught me at it and after the assembly was over she called me and made me kneel on the ground. I pleaded that it was an accident but she kept asking me how it happened. I did not want to expose the boy who pushed me and so remained silent.

Kneeling in the sun on the bare earth was painful and grazed my knees. I remember telling Ms. Phillips that she was unfair and I would show her! On returning home, I was taken to Vasuthatha's house so he could have a look at my knees. He casually asked me the name of the teacher. I told him and that was the end of the matter for me. The incident completely slipped out of my mind.

The next day while in class, I was summoned to the Principal's room. I was startled to see him sitting across the Principal's table. Ms. Phillips was standing to the left. Sister Lucia, the Principal, was a gentle Italian nun whom I later became very close to. She asked me what happened and I told her. She stroked my knees and asked if they hurt, probably because I winced. I shook my head. She told Ms. Phillips to see that I was not meted out any physically strenuous punishment since I was a sickly child and she said, "Well that's that, Dr. Vasu, you can be sure it will not happen again."

Ms. Phillips came and took me by the hand and led me out. Then she asked me, "Why did you not tell me who you were?" I stared blankly. She asked "Don't you know that your grandfather is the school doctor?" I just shook my head, it seems. I recall feeling terribly embarrassed by the whole episode! I am glad that Miss Phillips believed in my innocence in the whole matter.

The next year I went into Class 4A and Miss Phillips was the class teacher. We were an almost equal number of girls and boys in this class. In fact, this was the last year that the school continued as a co-educational institution. Miss Phillips made me the class monitor and I suspected that this was her way of ensuring that I did not squeal on her to my grandfather. During the morning interval she would give me her tea flask and ask me to accompany her to the staff room. I hated this duty. It was not an issue for me to carry the test books but she was afraid that it might be too much of a weight for me and so gave me the flask to carry. I got ragged quite a bit for this by my classmates.

It was not only the class students who were afraid of her. Even the seniors were afraid of her. She continued to teach in the school till her retirement, I think. This was the year that 'Chandi' or Chandni Ramkumar came into my class. Her father was a close friend of Appa. His wife had died of cancer and so Appa felt that having me as a friend would help Chandi cope with the loss. She was also an excellent student and the competition between us was keen and fun. I used to go home for lunch while she and her sisters had an 'ayah'[7] bring their lunch, serve them and sit around till they finished.

When school gave over, Chandi, her sister and two cousins walked back home with me. They lived two streets after mine. Chandi had this feeling of 'class' that I did not. There were a lot of girls who were very class conscious in school. I was always of a friendly nature and did not bother about whether it was a boy or girl, whether they were clever or not or poor or rich.

---

[7]   Ayah – Childcare assistant

One strong memory about the school was the kitchen with its rich and cloying smell of peanut toffee. I always knew when fresh toffee would be made and would beg and plead with Appamma to give me one anna[8] from which I would buy half anna's worth of toffee and put the other half anna into my piggy bank.

The year I got into school was the year my mother was pregnant with my youngest brother, Srikar. Appamma insisted that she go to Madras to Ammama's for the childbirth. I had just started school but was quite happy to be left behind with Thatha, Appamma, and Srinu (my uncle). Appa accompanied Amma but was to return immediately after leaving her at Madras.

The only issue was the fact that I had almost waist length thick hair which had to be braided into two plaits, each secured with black ribbon at the end and then tied across to the other plait. This was a school rule. I remember that on the day she was leaving, Amma oiled and plaited my hair tightly and strictly told me not to mess it up till the next day so that Appamma would be saved one day's struggle! With the dawn of day three the primary tension of Thatha, Appamma and Srinu was as to how the feat of plaiting my hair could be achieved. This was because Appamma was arthritic and her joints had no grip. In fact she could not bend her joints. So Srinu combed out my hair, Appamma parted it into two sections and I was so fussy that the parting should be absolutely straight that our house would be filled with my wails and screams of dissatisfaction every morning.

The way Appamma and Srinu would struggle to plait my hair every alternate day amused me greatly. Between them they would divide one section into three equal bunches – Appamma

---

[8]   Anna – currency then in use; 16 annas made a rupee

would hold one bunch and Srinu would put the second bunch over the one she was holding and then put the third bunch he was also holding, in a crisscross style and then each of them would pull at the ends of the bunches to tighten the plait and so it went on, till they reached the end. At the end, it was even trickier because the ribbon had to be added and plaited together and then tied into a knot at the end. Just as they thought they were finishing, the whole plait would slip loose and they would have to start all over again. My elder brother Kavi would just for the fun of it pitch in to help. Once this task was over, they would again warn me not to mess it up so that it could stay on till the next day! They could just as well have suggested that I be given a haircut till such time that Amma did not return but they must have been sick of seeing me bald for almost seven years and did not mind the tension and labor.

Amma's return was a great relief. I was very curious about my baby brother, but not jealous or insecure because he was so small and it made me feel important to care for him. I loved to make him laugh. Even in my fragile condition I would insist on carrying him on my hip just like Amma and Appamma were doing. Probably when Srikar was around 9 months or so, a 'boyi'[9] was hired. He must have been around 17 years old. Another old 'boyi' had brought him and vouched for his honesty. His job was to carry the baby, change his nappy, rock him to sleep in the cradle, and mind over him when he slept; he was like a nanny. Since I was so fond of the baby I would always tag along to watch over him whenever I didn't have school or studies.

I had my first conscious experience of sexual violence with this boyi. Every evening he would have to take the baby to the nearby park, hold his hand and make him walk around on the grass for some time. I was sent to mind over them. On the first

---

[9] Boyi – a live in household help from the Scheduled Caste

day itself this boy just set the baby free to romp around and then tried to misbehave with me; I felt very uncomfortable and pushing him off I got up to leave. On reaching home I did not know how to say what he had done and soon got immersed in my studies. The next day I was asked to go with them again and I refused. They tried persuading me but I was adamant.

A couple of days later, I was passing the coal shed on the way to our vegetable garden, the boyi pulled me into the shed and started tugging at my underpants. Just then Appamma happened to come by, probably to pick vegetables. Taking in everything at one glance she swiped her walking stick at him, pulled me away and shouted out for Amma, Appa and Thatha. They came and she told them what she saw. Appa and the others started bashing him and he was thrown out.

That was all, they went in, and washed their hands and feet. Amma told me that I should not allow anyone to touch me. Nothing more was discussed and it was as if nothing had happened at all. I don't even understand why I remember this – I couldn't express this at that young age but I felt violated in an unpleasant way and disliked it.

While it was tucked away in some corner of my brain I did not think about it any further. I recalled this incident when some years later, I told my mother that an uncle had tried to rape me and she told my father and the reaction was totally different. There was just silence, no action taken by my parents. Later on in life I understood there are two principles, unshakeable, I would say, in the whole social structure

- What happens within the family or extended family however horrible it may be, must never be exposed
- An untouchable like the Scheduled Caste boy should be mercilessly punished if he dares to touch an upper caste person.

I was a much loved child and the limitations that applied to girls normally in that day and age never applied to me. I had a lot of friends in school and all of them were from different castes[10] and religions. I had a lot of Muslims, Parsis, second generation Anglo Indians and Jews as friends. In fact, I also had one Seventh Day Adventist friend and improved my general knowledge by getting to know more about this particular Christian sect. I learnt a lot about various cultures and religions through my friends. Quite breezily I would often bring some of them home and slide my gaze away from the stormy looks of Appamma. Amma would gently shepherd us to the terrace if we wanted to play outdoor games or keep us in the outer verandah[11] if we wanted to remain indoors.

Since my outdoor activity stopped totally after my attack of rheumatic fever, it often used to be only sedentary indoor games. I loved playing the role of teacher if we were mimicking a classroom scenario. Interestingly, I was never enamored by the toy houses or tiny toy kitchenware that kids often played with. Most of the time when I was alone I was reading.

We had a wonderful library - the complete works of Shakespeare, Charles Dickens, and volumes of poetry which I devoured avidly. I lived in two worlds – one was the world of Shakespeare's Romeo and Juliet, Othello, As You Like It, Twelfth Night, Dickens' Oliver Twist, etc., Keats and Shelley's heavy, honeyed or light, fairylike poetry.

The other was my very orthodox Brahmin home where we had to collect cow dung from the road, mix it with some straw and water and then shape the mixture into flat cakes or balls and set to dry on the terrace to be used as fuel later, or help in roasting coffee beans in the quaint tin roaster, kept over a coal

---

[10]   Caste system in India
[11]   Verandah- courtyard

fire, or thread out semolina from the dough Appamma laid out before us, or shape biscuits for baking in the clay oven, or clean the dal and rice free of stones, or pick out leaves from the kitchen garden for boiling and extracting juice to prepare our hair oil or roll out papads[12] - it was endless, the number of chores we did and I enjoyed every minute of it. Papad making and pickle making (of mangoes) were major activities in our house. It used to be done once a year and for this my father's cousins' wives used to turn up because Appamma was mother-in-law for them too in the absence of their own mother-in-law. It was one more activity that I looked forward to eagerly. The kneading of the papad dough and then the pounding of it in a huge stone grinder was fascinating.

Amma's hands were small and delicate but my aunts' hands were tough and large. They would empty the flour into a huge bowl and then Appamma used to pour castor oil and add salt and some other spices. She would then take the pounding stick and with her arthritic hands do the first pound, then my aunts would take over from her and with the nine yard saris neatly tucked, they would pound, sweating and grunting when the vigor and time increased. I played the very important role of keeping a thin towel ready to go and wipe the sweat from their brow so that it did not fall into the dough.

Once Appamma checked the consistency, the dough would be transferred from the grinding stone to a 'thambalam[13]'. They would break for a meal and then Appamma would allow me to also help. With palms smeared with castor oil, we would make small balls of the dough and throw them into another thambalam. Once all the balls were made, Appamma would

---

[12]   Papads – crispies made with lentils
[13]   Thambalam – large serving tray made of brass or silver in the old days

once again roll out the first papad. While Amma and my aunts rolled out the regular papads, I was given a small rolling board and pin to roll out small papads for myself. We would dry them in the shade first and then in the sun. My aunts would be given their share of papads by Appamma. She sometimes also gifted them saris.

The other major event was that of pickling mangoes. It would be in summer and since it was vacation time, I would accompany Appa and Amma to Monda Market[14] to buy green mangoes. There was one shop we would regularly go to where we were always welcomed with a cheerful greeting and a beautiful bantering bargain would start between my parents and the vendors. Once the price was fixed, we would all sit on the ground and pick out the mangoes. Some calculation followed and then the vendors would take out a cutting board and hatchet-like knife and chop the whole mangoes into pieces for pickling. We would take them home and Appa used to carry the bag since it was heavy.

My aunts would arrive around noon and then the tub would be washed thoroughly, half filled with water and the mango pieces emptied into the tub. They would be quickly washed and removed so that the water did not get absorbed. The pieces would be put on to a huge piece of cotton cloth and wiped dry. The chili powder would already have been pounded by two women helpers. The other ingredients would all be ready. Appa, Amma and I would have gone to the oil pressing unit and got freshly pressed gingelly[15] oil. I watched from a distance because Appamma was particular that the chili powder should not fall on my face and distress me. As I recall,

---

[14]   Monda market – wholesale market for all groceries, vegetables, etc. in Secunderabad

[15]   Gingelly oil – oil extracted from sesame seeds

our home was a veritable cottage industry. While I enjoyed the whole process, I did not enjoy this type of mango pickle. I liked the sweet mango pickle of which some would be made and kept aside for me. Three types of pickle would be made – one was the basic 'avakkai' [16] The other was 'bellamavakkai' [17] and one more was the 'cobbaravakkai' [18].

The next day's lunch would be just pickle and rice and curd rice – so that the experts, that is, Appa and Appamma, taste and say what remedies are needed before it is too late. The pickle would have to mull for at least a week before we could eat it. The first time we ate it was also a ritual. On an evening when everyone was at home, Amma would ladle hot cooked rice onto a big stainless steel plate and pour gingelly oil onto Appamma's cupped palm, who in turn would pour it around onto the rice and then Amma would mix the pickle in the three foot jar and ladle some out onto the rice. Appamma would carefully mix the pickle into the hot rice, literally scalding her fingers in the process.

All of us, including Thatha would be sitting round in a circle. Appamma would then take a handful, ball it in her palm and give the first into Appa's palm. He was considered the connoisseur as far as food and taste were concerned and if he nodded, Thatha and the rest of us would, according to age get served. I liked the ritual but not the food. The pickle was too sour for my taste. I remember, on one occasion, Amma realized that we were running out of cooked rice and she quickly set another pot of rice to cook on the stove and everyone waited patiently for it to cook. After all of us finished, Amma would ladle out some rice and pickle for herself and Appamma, who

---

[16] Avakkai – Mustard flavoured mango pickle
[17] Bellamavakkai - Mustard and jaggery flavoured mango pickle
[18] Cobbaravakkai – Coconut and mustard flavoured mango pickle

would put a ball of the mixed rice onto Amma's palm and throw a ball into her mouth from a distance, so that her fingers did not touch her lips. We all grew up pouring water, coffee or anything from a glass into our mouths.

Touching our mouth with our hands or any container to our lips while drinking something was not allowed since it was 'Yecchhe'[19] and was frowned upon. I don't remember our having any teacups or rimless glasses in our home. There was so much of orthodox Brahmin family on one side with 'devasams'[20] and 'madi'[21] and on the other, there would be sudden visits of the 'communists' who were underground and I think also used our home as a hideout.

The memories of the communists' visits are very hazy because I was too young. But I do remember that these men would come in very quietly and Amma would have to cook so much and they would eat like they hadn't eaten for days together. Thinking back, it must be true that they really hadn't eaten for days. The devasams, I hated, because such a fuss would be on from the previous day itself. Thatha's and Appamma's clothes would be washed by Amma and hung on a high string in the back verandah. None of us were to touch it. Once Kavi and I did, just for fun and Amma had to pull them down and wash them all over again. When we saw this I swore never to repeat such a prank.

A male cook would come to cook on the day of the devasam, and my paternal uncles and aunts (who were cousins of Appa, and their families) would attend the rituals and partake of the meal. Those of us going to school or work would go but when we returned we had to eat the food cooked

---

[19]   Yecchhe – defiled with spit
[20]   Devasam – death anniversary ritual
[21]   Madi – not to be defiled by touch

for the ritual. Everyone in the house liked the food but I hated it. From a very early age I hated wholly sour and wholly sweet things. Only a mixed sweet and sour taste was to my liking. I also did not like spicy food and absolutely hated too many dishes at any meal. There used to be a particular type of food cooked at 'devasams' that I never liked. In fact I would always hate festival food because everything was sour and spicy and there was this rule that we should taste all the dishes made and finish the food on our plates.

I think I have a problem of hyperacidity which nobody understood. It has always been a problem. In fact, I add a dash of jaggery or sugar to my curries and chutneys. These tastes I realize now, do indicate something about the status of our bodies, but we tend to ignore the signals. Just as Amma used to try to force me to eat the type of food I did not like, I see that most mothers force their kids to eat what they have an aversion for.

Alongside all this activity, Thatha was ever so keen that I read as widely as possible and once when he saw how irritated I was to find that some pages were missing from the book 'The Count of Monte Cristo' which I was reading, he decided that he must give me a present. And one fine day there was a parcel from the postman for me – the complete works of Alexandre Dumas. They were an Oxford publication and came all the way from the U K. None of my friends were book addicts like me.

I lived in so many worlds. I had my book world which I did not share with anyone. I had another different world with my immediate family. I had one world each for friends of different religions. They could never be mixed and I felt comfortable in keeping them separate. I remember that once I had gone to the home of an Anglo-Indian friend during lunch time. Their food smelt odd and I thought that is how English people eat. Like the Anglo-Indian friends believed about themselves, I also believed that they were more English than Indian and the smell I found strange was the English smell! When the food was served on my plate I could not touch it and felt too shy to ask for bread and butter. And so I starved, while my friend Pamela ate. She told me that they were eating fried bacon and bread. The bread was fried in the same grease and I could not tolerate the smell.

I made a mental note to go home and ask Srinu what bacon was! He had a lot of Anglo-Indian friends and was worldly wise about many matters. I think he had also tried out the various kinds of cuisine. He had Chinese, Parsi, Anglo-Indian, and Muslim friends.

The other embarrassment I have about myself to date is my inability to eat with a fork and knife. I can only use my right hand and if there is an envy I have it is that of ambidextrous persons. Even now, I feel that everyone is surprised at my clumsiness with the knife and fork. I can only eat with my right hand.

I had many friends, all different from each other. Chandi, her elder sister Rani and her cousin, Rekha, children of parents who were friends of my parents formed one group. Then I had Pamela, Honoria, Patricia, and Maria, children of the family chemist and dentist, and a few odd ones. Then I had Tasleem, Samaira and Sameena from Salimchacha'[22]s family.

My friendship with the girls from Salimchacha's family lasted for a fairly long time. The story is that Salimchacha lived in the street parallel to ours and my father had this sudden notion of buying the house since we had moved house twice already and it was quite a pain packing, moving, unpacking

---

[22]   Salimchacha – Salim uncle

and settling down. For me it was one great joyride since I anyway did not do any work and it was great fun to sit either on the bundles in a bullock cart or if it was hot, inside a Tonga[23] and then discover what would become my favorite places in the new house.

Coming back to the house we never bought, it was a house with four or five small rooms – not as airy and spacious as the one we were living in. I didn't like it and hoped secretly that we would not have to move. The house we lived in the longest according to my memory, was so lovely, with the pillars and backyard and vast terrace where our neighbour's mango tree fell on one side, there were the cow dung cakes used as fuel in our home, drying in one corner. There were long cracks running across the length of the terrace and they had been filled with cement by Srinu. Most of this kind of work used to be done by the men in the family and the cottage industry thrived on the labor of the women and children.

Thatha flatly turned down the idea of buying Salimchacha's house saying that he did not believe that we should own a house by taking a loan from somewhere else and he was just paying Rs.75 per month as rent. In the process of exchange of talks between Appa and Salimchacha, I became friends with the girls in his family, who also studied in St. Hilda School.

Salimchacha continued to live there once Appa declined to buy the house and it became a new haunt for me. Immediately after school I would change into a skirt and run off to his house. The relationships there puzzled me till I became an adult and understood relationships. Samaira was Taslim's paternal aunt and younger than her, Zulfi was Samaira's cousin and so on. There were so many people living in that house and it was the

---

23   Tonga – Indian horse carriage

biggest joint family I had ever seen, living under one roof; it was amazing that everything went on so quietly and smoothly.

We used to play in the lane outside the house and when we went in, tired, after much skipping and other games, Taslim's mother would offer me a warm half of a bun with sugar and butter spread on top. At first I refused but when she said that it was vegetarian, I relented and took it. Even to this day I can taste the softness and lightness of the bun in my mouth. Of course, I never mentioned this at home because Appamma would have made me scrub my tongue and innards out with ash and sand!

Opposite Salimchacha's house lived a Tamil Brahmin family – consisting of father, mother, and daughter. The father was well-known in the neighborhood. I remember this family as an unsmiling family. All three of them had tight, pursed lips and frowns on their foreheads anytime I saw them. The daughter would never come to play with us but she would lean on her compound wall and watch us. She would wait till I passed close enough and whisper 'Chichi[24], a Brahmin girl playing with Muslims.' She was older than us and 'passed' the age of playing hide and seek, etc. Zulfi, Taslim's uncle was maybe around 19 – 20 years old and fair and 'handsome.' He would just stand on the sidewalk, arms folded and watch us with a tolerant smile. We generally ignored him and carried on with our games.

One day, this girl called me inside her house compound and handed me a small rolled up piece of paper instructing me to give it to Zulfi 'chachu.[25]'I very faithfully did so. The next day she did the same thing and while playing I would hand over the note to him. This became a daily feature. One day

---

[24]   Chichi – an expression similar to –'tchch' in English

[25]   Chachu – Hindi / Urdu for father's younger brother, uncle

when I went to play, there was much excitement that Zulfi chachu's 'nikaah[26]' was going to take place soon. I was also excited.

One day Taslim told me in school not to come to play in the evening. About 4 – 5 days later I learnt that the Brahmin girl had jumped from the terrace of their house and broken her spine and what had made her take this step was the news of Zulfi chachu's nikaah. I couldn't believe this. I learnt that the notes she sent through me were 'I love you' notes. He had never looked at her or sent her any notes. Her family knew this and was terribly ashamed.

The funny part of the whole story was that I very righteously went and demanded of Zulfi as to why he encouraged her and he laughed and said that he didn't even know the notes were from her, in fact he thought they were from me. It seems that he showed Salimchacha the notes, who asked Taslim to inform if it was me, and she said that it was not my handwriting; then, it seems her aunt Samaira saw it and disclosed whose handwriting it was! This incident was slowly wiped out of our minds since the family shifted home. In my childhood friendships I found that as we kept growing, we grew out of our friendships too and moved on to a new set of friends.

Healthwise, I had been well for some time and it seemed like fate would not leave me in peace. One morning I woke up and could not get out of bed. I tried moving my legs and the knees hurt like mad. I could not sit up on my own. I cried out and Amma and Appa looked at my legs and despaired. Appa called up Doctor Chinnana and Srinu went to get him home. He saw me and said that it was rheumatic fever. He said that it was going to be a long illness and my diet was 'kandipappu,

---

[26]   Nikaah- engagement ceremony

rottey[27]'. It was a truly long illness and tiring – being bedridden for over a month.

I was in Class 5 and this illness was just before my annual examinations. I insisted that I would write the examination and that the principal should be conveyed the same information. Appa did the needful. My knees were still swollen and I was suffering from fever but Appa used to carry me, seat me in the car, drive me down and then carry me to the ante room of the Principal where a special seating arrangement had been made for me. I did not even have the energy to read the question paper. The questions had to be read out, and I would dictate the answer to my scribe. I still managed to get first class marks in this examination.

During the entire vacation following the examinations, I was partly sick and partly recovering. It was yet another debilitating illness. I lost all desire to eat and thought I would never be able to walk again. The prospect of walking like Amma when I was not even 12 terrified me. From this illness onwards it was my fortitude and patience that were being put to the test, not my parents' only. I thought that I would probably be bedridden once again. But even at that age, I did not allow my family to see my fear. They had already borne enough of my illness. Thankfully, Dr. Chinnana once again proved to be the miracle man and I recovered. There were a lot of restrictions on my diet and activity. The rheumatic fever had caused a murmur in my heart and so I was not allowed to do anything that required physical strain. Even my normal walk had to be slowed down. I could not expose myself to anyone with any kind of common cold or cough or fever. As a result I hardly got exposed to crowded places.

---

[27]   Kandipappu, rottey – lentils and roti or greaseless bread

Five months later, just as I was setting out for school, I went to the bathroom. When I pulled down my panties, I found fresh blood stains on it and blood dripping from me. I was so petrified I yelled for Srinu. He came and seeing my condition, asked me to wait and called Amma. She came and then gently washed me; she went and brought a pad of cotton and layered it onto a fresh panty which she pulled up my legs and patted the cotton wad comfortably in place. Then she said that I need not go to school for the day.

Appamma asked Amma to spread a mat on the floor in the room that Amma used to sit in for four days every month, eating and sleeping there, then entering the main house only after having a 'head bath' on the fifth day. I would not be allowed to touch her and if I did, I would have to be washed with 'Ganga water' before entering the house. When Appamma said I too had to go and sit there, I screamed.

She quickly asked Amma to spread the mat in the front verandah and told me, 'Don't come near me.' I promptly made a beeline for her and sat on her lap. She laughed helplessly but did not push me away. Instead, she hugged me to her and fondly scolded me, 'Lankini[28], Kaikeyi[29], thank God you have grown up...we were so worried that you would not mature at all. She wanted to have a ceremony, inviting the neighborhood to celebrate my 'coming of age,' and I screamed that there would be nothing of the sort.

---

[28] Lankini-female resident of Lanka, the kingdom of Ravana the demon of the Indian epic Ramayana. Lankini was characterized by a wild temper which was considered unfeminine

[29] Kaikeyi- fourth and favourite wife of Dasaratha in Ramayana known for her stubbornness and heartlessness in using her beauty to persuade the king to send Rama to the forest for 12 years

'It is too early, but nevertheless it has started,' my parents said. Dr. Chinnana was told about the development and he also heaved a sigh of relief; he gave some medicines to relieve my stomach cramps. As always, I slept on the floor in the central hall along with my brothers and Srinu; Amma slept on a cot. Thatha had a room to himself which Appamma used during the day and Appa and Amma had a separate bedroom. Once Srinu got married he got a separate bedroom.

From the first time I got my periods till Srinu lived with us, he would always come and wake me up once at night with a neatly prepared wad of cotton and take me to the bathroom to change. He would stand outside while I went into the bathroom. I would remove the soiled pad and roll it in the piece of paper which Srinu handed me and then take the fresh pad to use. The soiled ones I would place in a corner of the bathroom above the coal stack and when the boiler was lit for heating bath water, I would drop the wads of soiled cotton into the boiler tunnel – the smell was terrible.

Asha, my sister was either in Delhi or Madras and she had written me a long letter detailing the whole process of menstruation and what I should do and reassuring me not to be afraid and shocked – but the letter arrived a month after I had started my periods. I treasured this letter for several years because it showed how much she loved me and was concerned about me, that she wanted to try and prevent for me the shock and trauma a girl undergoes when she first sees blood streaming down her legs.

When I see the comfort women have today, in terms of going through the monthly 'curse', it makes me jealous! It was such a torture managing that uncomfortable bundle of cotton between my legs every 22 days and despair at not knowing how to dispose of the soiled ones. I remember that many times when I went to Madras for the vacation I would carry the newspaper wrapped soiled bundles in a bag for two or three days, searching for a roadside dustbin where I could drop the stuff. I used to be so scared that some passerby would catch me in the act and scold or punish me!

I think that my non-conformist attitude was evident from the nicknames I was given by Appamma and Thatha. Appamma used to generally call me Lankini and Kaikeyi whether she wanted to be endearing or scolding and Thatha had given me the nickname 'gypsy.' The conclusion I can draw from this is that I was either a terrible shrew, villain or as wild as a gypsy!

During my childhood I was quite often puzzled by the behavior of the men in the family and it is only around three decades back that this behavior got a name – domestic violence. All of a sudden, Thatha would start shouting at Amma and then start beating her, and more vigorously, the floor around her, with his walking stick. He was a small made man certainly shorter than her by almost a foot and she was big made whereas he was puny. It was a ludicrous scene.

It is such decades since both of them have left this world but I always wondered why she did not stop him browbeating her. All of a sudden Thatha would put a few clothes into a cloth bag and walk off down the street to the garage of one Dr. Desai's house. Amma would shout at Appa and Amma and also pack a few clothes, a kerosene stove, and cooking vessels and follow Thatha. Appa and Amma would walk down with some food later and then both of them would prostrate themselves at the feet of my grandparents but to no avail. They did not relent and come back. They would stay for a few days in that garage.

Appamma would make some attempt to cook but be quite relieved when she sighted the food that Amma unfailingly packed and delivered punctually at the doorstep. The beating would stop immediately both of them went off to the Desai shed and set up their temporary home. This was a very strange phenomenon which puzzled me tremendously. I did not find Appa beating Amma except much later, when his drinking assumed serious proportions and he became really violent during his drinking sprees.

When I questioned Amma about this kind of behavior on the part of men and why the women did not hit back, Amma would just shush me up. These incidents of violence always upset me and I would run to the most comforting person among all of them – Srinu. He was a pillar of strength, reassurance and affection for all of us children. He got married only after my sister Asha got married. He was devoted to Amma and us. I heard much later that the family felt it may be misconstrued by society. Once he got married Appa pressurized Srinu to move out and set up a home on his own so there was no room for any misunderstanding. Once they moved out and had a child Appamma also moved in with them. As I grew older and saw the depiction of the 'Bhabi – Devar[30]' relationship in Hindi cinema, I realized that in my family this relationship between Amma and Srinu was so close and friendly. What an emotionally luxurious life I had led through my childhood despite my long bouts of ill health.

I was a thin, small framed girl. As I neared 13, there was not much difference I felt in myself, except the sprouting of hair on legs and arms and pubic region. Just as my hair on the head was thick so also the hair all over the rest of my body was thick and black. It filled me with shame and discomfort. To top it all,

---

[30] Bhabhi – Devar relationship – relationship between a woman and her husband's younger brother

Amma decided that I should be like the other modern girls and would stitch knee length frilly skirts and cute collared blouses.

She went to great care in choosing the material and if possible stitched them herself. If she was too busy she got Jeeriah the tailor in the adjacent street to stitch them. I would get into a frenzy that I wanted the regular 'pavadai[31]' and she could not fathom why I did not like the kind of skirts that others were wearing. When I pointed to the hair on my legs she simply said it was quite normal. She would pull me to her and dress me up every evening and push me off to play. Most often my friends didn't even notice, since there was so much else to do, but I was always very self-conscious.

My friendship with Chandi at this time came to an all-time low because Chandi was already very adult in her thinking. Sometimes when she talked about it with me I was quite frankly puzzled because I did not understand most of what she was saying. I think she liked to shock me and said a lot of things just in order to shock me!

My new friend was Lalita Naidu who lived just down the same street. Her father and mine used to play tennis together some evenings. I was quite tall for my age but Lalita was taller than me. She may have been a year older than me. Her father was a Telugu Hindu, mother was a Goan Christian. Jayanti the older sister was a petite, pretty young woman who fascinated me!

Lalita's two older brothers were again tall and lanky. The older brother Deepak was a typically handsome chap, like the famous film actor Gregory Peck. He was the first person I fell in love with – and he didn't even know I existed! This was something that did not matter to me – it was just one of many feelings I had and feelings at that age were so varied, so

---

[31]   Pavadai – skirt from waist to ankles

fleeting and so many. I was one of those rare Brahmin girls who actually wore knee length skirts and a collared waist length blouse in those days. The hula hoop was a new craze and I insisted on Thatha getting me one, because Lalita had one and we both would hula hoop down the street from my house to hers and back to mine.

Then there was the romance of Lalita's sister, Jayanti and a local cricket hero and it was such excitement to watch him swagger down the street every evening and then both of them walk hand in hand up the street, once they were engaged to be married. I would be thrilled beyond words if he smiled and said hello to me. Thanks to him and Lalita my autograph book was filled with personalized greetings from famous cricketers like Frank Worrel, Gary Sobers, Neil Harvey, Richie Benaud and so many others!

The fun of sitting in Lalita's house when her mother brought home two bags of vegetables and dumped them into a tub of water and ordered us both to rinse them well and sort them out on sheets of newspaper is a simple chore that brings a smile to my face even now. This washing and sorting of vegetables is a pleasure that is ever fresh.

How can I put into words the thrill of sneaking Lalita up to our terrace and then stealthily going down into the storeroom where the pickles were kept and fish out two pieces of sweet mango pickle for Lalita? If Appamma caught me she would scold Lalita and immediately send her home saying she is a bad influence on me! One day Lalita brought a small silver figurine of Krishna and gave it to me saying it was for our puja room. I proudly marched off to Appamma and gave her the figurine saying what a nice girl Lalita was. Appamma harrumphed, 'Oh – that is only till she gets caught trying to get you to steal pickle once again. Then she'll take back the 'vigraham.[32]' It was so true – a few days later Lalita did ask me to get some pickle and I said that Appamma would skin me, so, sorry. She promptly said, 'Bring me back my Krishna figurine. I want it back.' The friendship with Lalita kept waxing and waning and she is among those 'lifetime friends' that I have though we live on totally different continents.

We were all at the age when our sexuality was just about awake. Our menstrual pains, bodies growing, body hair springing out, pimples and acne (luckily I did not go through that trauma, except for the odd pimple jutting out once in a while) went hand in hand with new feelings and sensations. As we grew, our studies also became deeper and more complex. Health Science and Nature Study gave way to Biology, Physics and Chemistry. Math was tough, with Coordinate Geometry, Trigonometry and Calculus being included. These were areas where even Thatha or Appa could not help us. However, the rigor of the math I had learnt till then was such that it became fairly easy for me to grasp the complexities of High School math.

As I recall, the sudden entry of boys into our talk, and our thoughts, just happened. A few years earlier we used to laugh at the giggling, blushing Beverly and Shirley and Kulsum – and suddenly we found ourselves doing the same thing! That age is a heady one. There is pain, gawkiness, breathless excitement, and a feeling of being able to do anything! That top of the world feeling is priceless!

I would say that I was fortunate to have parents and family that clearly laid rules of what was not permissible. I found that many girls did not have that discipline and nonnegotiable rules and I could see what it did to them at that point of time and later on also. I was more into my studies than anything else but

---

[32] Vigraham - idol

enjoyed helping my friends by passing love notes and making anonymous telephone calls on their behalf.

The telephone had just come to Hyderabad and we were one of the first families to get a phone connection. Since there were not all that many phone connections it was not a problem for me to remember telephone numbers. I would call up a number on behalf of my friend and say, 'if you want to see your dream girl come to Marredpalli garden at 4 'o' clock tomorrow evening'. This was a real comedy of errors. My friend was a boarder in the school and she had a crush on a boy who lived down the lane from the school and studied in St. Stephen's School. So the phone message I was giving was on her behalf. But it seems that he was 'following' me and he thought that I reciprocated. The boarding school girls would come to the said park for an evening walk duly escorted by a nun, of course, and I would join them in the walk, strolling beside my special friend. This boy and his set of friends would walk on the opposite side of the park, trying to look very indifferent.

One day I called up this boy to give a similar message and did not know that their house had an extension phone and after I said what I wanted to, I heard a female voice screeching at me 'don't you have any shame, what's your name, I'll complain to your parents…' I quickly placed the phone back on its cradle, panic stricken, and decided to confide in Amma; I told her everything. The next day she called up the boy's house and asked to speak with the lady of the house and gave a piece of her mind and asked that they keep their boy reined in. I was glad my mother knew when to believe me.

The most exciting event of my teens was my sister Asha's wedding. Appa, Amma and I were driving to Dr. Chinnana's and were on Clover Bridge and I heard Appa saying, 'Let us fix the wedding for May then. You talk with your mother'.

Amma said yes and I immediately piped up with the question 'whose wedding?' Amma said, 'Asha's' and 'you don't go about telling anyone this.' I did not remember much about Asha in my childhood because she was either busy with her friends or used to be sent off to Delhi to my aunt and then Madras to Ammama. I was so busy with my own life and had no time to be curious about anyone else! When I heard Appa and Amma in the car I wondered why the discussion was taking place in such hushed tones between my parents.

It was a practice for Appa to take off in the car if he had something confidential to discuss. I wondered at my parents' decision to get her married; but these puzzled me only momentarily and I was off into my own world. She was to marry Rajamama, Amma's youngest brother and one of my favourite uncles. He was a humorous person, very intelligent and it was said that he used to sit under the street lamp and study for his graduate examinations when Ammama moved to Madras. The story, as told by him, goes that when Asha was just a kid, he had vowed that he would only marry her. It was also a custom in families from our caste to give one daughter in marriage to the maternal uncle.

The wedding was a grand affair. She was probably the first in that generation of our family to get married. Besides, of course, she was everybody's favourite. I never knew that there was so much silver in the house, till Appamma started taking them out and deciding what should be given to Asha. The silverware was given to Amma at the time she got married and some of it was what Appamma got when she got married. There was a gold waistband and a ruby necklace and then there was this hunt for genuine, high quality blue tinted diamonds for the bride's ear rings. Some diamonds were selected and then checked out by two persons – one was a jeweler and the other was Oppuuncle a close friend of my parents and professor in

Chemistry at the State University. Assured that they were the rarest of the rare, the best were selected and given for setting in gold. Amma used to take the diamonds and go to the goldsmith and sit while they were being set. If it was not done by the end of the day she would bring back the pouch and take it the next day.

The family tailors were commissioned to report every morning and stitch all our clothes in the rear verandah of our house. On the one hand jewelry was being made, and on the other, stainless steel utensils were being bought, silver, brass and copper ware being readied; the copper boiler and matching copper tub fascinated me and I vowed that I would also insist that I be given a similar one when I got married. I accompanied Amma and Appamma to the sari shop in Market Bazar. We bought lovely Kanchi[33] silk saris for Asha and I remember one delicious mango yellow sari with a magenta border and small mangoes embroidered with gold and magenta thread all over and a splendid magenta and gold pallav. I was very excited that she would look so beautiful in that sari. Asha was a very beautiful woman. My excitement was boundless just imagining her in all that wedding finery. I was allowed two sets of pavadai since I was related to both the bride and groom. I got a lovely light chocolate with orange and gold border pavadai from my parents and a light cream with green and gold checks and green and gold border pavadai from Ammama. Since I had 'matured,' I had to also wear a 'davani.[34]' I remember the beautiful ruby jewelry set Asha was given by Amma and for many years it filled me with envy!

---

[33]   Kanchi – saris woven in Kancheepuram, Tamilnadu

[34]   Davani – a three metre stole tucked into the pavadai at the waist and draped like a sari across the front – worn by adolescent girls in south India before they moved on to wearing the full sari.

A lot of stuff was bought – the dower Asha was to carry to her marital home, gifts for almost all the relatives, helpers and close friends. Snacks were being prepared since it was decided that the wedding would be held at home. Seshumama planned that the rose garlands for the bride and groom would be flown in from Madras. An Iyengar cook was hired for a month before the wedding since everybody was busy with the wedding preparations. I recall that one of my several uncles behaved very badly with his wife and the argument reached such a peak that he started beating her. She was weeping and he dragged her out of the house. Once they left, everyone resumed whatever they were doing.

This kind of beating up was peculiar to my mind but a very common sight during my childhood and that was when I seem to have made up my mind that I would never let a man touch a hair on my head. As I have grown older of course I have seen this kind of wife beating being passed off with a comment like 'if the husband does not beat his wife who will?' Why should anyone beat a woman was my question and it has made me happy that the Domestic Violence legislation was enacted many decades later!

The wedding day grew closer and it was a three day celebration. The wedding was on May 21 but the 'Jaanavasam[35]' was on the evening of May 20th. I remember wearing the green and gold pavadai with matching blouse and a 'davani.' There was the typical 'nadaswaram' music band leading the procession which consisted mostly of men and children like me. We walked from our house to the Anjaneya temple on the 4th street. Chandi and I were on either side of Srinu and somewhere along the walk, I took off my davani and gave to Srinu to hold; he tied it on his head like a turban.

---

[35] Jaanavasam – ceremony on wedding eve

In south India wearing a davani was compulsory once a girl started menstruating. So taking it off in the middle of the road was an unspeakable act. But I couldn't be bothered and the procession was mostly of men and nobody took notice. Later on, when I started observing other girls of my age I saw that since they were all sprouting breasts threatening to burst forth the davani was meant to cover the chest. I was happily flat chested and so it was superfluous in my case!

Coming back to the 'Jaanavasam', there must have been at least a hundred people for the occasion which ended with a dinner. The next day was the wedding and it took place in our house compound with a shamiana[36] stretching to at least 200 yards of the road. Nobody complained, probably because there were no families we did not know that would want to use the road. I felt that the whole of Secunderabad was at the wedding. I was wearing the chocolate and orange pavadai and did not make a pretense of looking big by wearing the 'davani' because I was entranced by the grandeur of the whole function. Everyone was in silk; even the men wore silk 'veshtis[37]' and 'angavastrams[38]'.

There was the nadaswaram playing songs specific for each ritual. A well-known radio singer and a close friend of Amma, called Lakshmi Senthil was singing special 'unjal[39]' songs. For this I remember Asha and Rajamama sitting on the 'unjal' and being swung gently while Lakshmi sang.

---

[36] Shamiana – cloth tent put up for big functions and popular even now.

[37] Veshti – four yard long cloth with the width of a sari which south Indian men wrap around their waist

[38] Angavastram – scarf to go with the veshti to cover the chest

[39] Unjal - swing

The other ritual that stayed on in my mind is when Appa sat on a sack of rice and Asha sat on his lap and the 'kanyadanam[40]' took place. One more ritual was when Rajamama held Asha's foot and placed it on a stone, I don't know the significance of this, but it was quaint. Of course the 'Kasi yatra[41]' was so hilarious with the bridegroom walking off with an umbrella, a stick and a coconut shell (as a bowl), and then the bride's father went and beseeched him to return and marry his daughter! Rajamama looked very cute with kohl lined eyes and a beauty spot on his cheek. I had a fever by the end of the day and wished everyone would just go off, leaving the home in peaceful silence.

After a few days, Rajamama, Asha and, I think, Ammama left for Madras and it was all quiet once again. Asha stayed on in Madras and Rajamama returned to Madurai where he was working in VWS, Northern Roadways. Asha, I think, went to President's College, Madras, to complete her B.A. Honours in English. I don't remember exactly when, but some months later Amma, Kavi, Srikar and I went to Madras and we were to later accompany Asha along with Ammama to Madurai and help her set up her home. What I remember is that Asha was pregnant and our tickets were booked. On the supposed to be 'D' day Ammama and Amma cooked a whole lot of food, filled the silver and stainless steel 'kujas[42]' with water and we all set off to the railway station to board the train.

We happily boarded and went off grandly to the berths numbered on our tickets under Amma's guidance. Some

---

[40] Kanyadanam – giving away of (donating) a girl (daughter)
[41] Kasiyatra – undertaking a journey to Kasi the ultimate pilgrimage for Hindus who want to give up all material desires and possessions
[42] Kuja - flask

people were already sitting there. We tried explaining that the seats were ours and were told that it was not so and then Amma took out our tickets and the person occupying the seats took out his and he spotted the big goof up. Our tickets were for the next day.

Ammama insisted that we travel somehow on that day since it was auspicious and we cannot get another one till a week later. It seems unbelievable even now but we all got bundled into the unreserved compartment with the entire luggage and it was one of many uncomfortable train journeys I have undertaken in my life.

We sat on the floor of the compartment and Amma served out dinner for us. After that, she cleaned up the floor and spread newspaper so that Asha could stretch herself. Poor thing, she was really in bad shape. The train was running really late and we were all totally tired by the time we reached Madurai.

Since Rajamama had just taken up a new house on rent, we were supposed to go and help in getting it into shape. A family friend of Ammama had arranged to have us refresh ourselves at his home, have lunch and then go over to our 'home.'

I seem to have been living in a world of my own most of the time, my brain crammed with my studies, the impressions of the hordes of books I read and impressions of life around me. So I was quite dim when it came to simple observation of my immediate surroundings at any moment of time – in a sense it seemed almost as if I was distanced from what was happening around me. The following incident is an illustration.

In this house in Madurai, I was passing Asha who was near the terrace wall and she was swaying helplessly – she told me to tell someone that she was feeling dizzy. So I went to Amma, told her, 'Asha is feeling dizzy,' and walked on to continue with whatever I was doing. It seems they just about managed to rescue Asha tipping off the parapet wall. I got a solid scolding and they said that I always lived in a world of my own and would never change.

Then Amma recalled when once, in our Marredpalli home she was outside talking with one of her friends living down the street about something important, she asked me to 'go and see the milk.' Which when paraphrased, means to make sure it does not boil over. I just saw the milk and went back to whatever I was doing. Amma happened to return to the kitchen and the milk had boiled over, running down the cooking platform onto the floor. When she came and asked me what did I do – it seems I looked puzzled and she said 'about the milk' and I said 'you asked me to see it and I saw it!' This is a story that would be repeated over and over again to point out my sense of detachment to the world around me!

On the whole, I liked my stay in Madurai. All my favourite people were there, except Appa and I obviously missed him a lot and wrote him long letters which he preserved till a year before he died. He gave them to me when he was staying with me. I realized when I read these letters, that I had this tendency to be very theatrical in my expressions of love for anybody. It was probably the influence of all the fiction I used to read. My letters to someone I liked would go something like this...'my dearest, darlingest ..... I really miss you so much so much I can't breathe.......lots and lots of love from the bottom of my heart...' This was uniform, to mother, father, grandfather, friend (girl or boy).

Once we got back to Hyderabad leaving the much married Asha and Rajamama in their new home it was back to the grind for me. There was a lot of studying to do since the math and Science syllabi, while connected to whatever we had studied in the lower classes, were much higher and we had to grapple with new and difficult terms and concepts. For me, this was the phase of Newton's Laws of Motion, Pythagoras theorem, Sulphuric Acid formulae, along with Coordinate Geometry, Calculus, Trigonometry and Bible Knowledge! So much information we had to absorb; and it had to be done all on our own, because our parents did not have much knowledge about the subject and there were not many teachers outside of our school who could be hired as private tutors.

One interesting part of our school curriculum was music and in high school, our music classes took a very exciting twist, because a tall, fair, wide eyed, slender nun used to play the piano and sing also. We would all go totally out of tune, but she merely smiled, hopelessly shaking her head. It did not seem to matter to her because her mind was filled with the music she played – or so we thought! Later we came to realize that she had other thoughts occupying her mind – thoughts that people who are wedded to the church should not even entertain. We always wondered among ourselves in whispers how and why she became a nun, because she was so beautiful, cheerful and full of fun.

True to our doubts, one day she did not turn up at all and we were told there would not be any more music lessons till further notice. There were whisperings among the teachers and the nuns. We soon came to know that our music teacher had left the church in order to marry her boyfriend! We realized that the envelopes she asked us to take and place in the church were actually love letters. This was amazing coordination and networking in an age when even landline telephone connections were rare!

While I had my share of excitement in school, with friends, there was a lot happening around me and away from me too. My uncle, Rajan had married a Christian, Matilda, and she was a nurse in the hospital where he was sent for treatment for some illness. I don't remember when they got married though the occasion made an impression because it raised the tempers of the elders in my family. Actually, I hardly saw him. The marriage was not acceptable to Appamma and both of them were barred from entering our house.

In the same year that my brother Srikar was born, Rajan and Matilda's son Jaikar was born. For some reason he was called Puttu and it seems when he was born his legs were twisted oddly. Amma and Appa went and saw him and it seems Amma used to go and massage his legs every day. She was very fond of him, in fact more than she was of Srikar.

I was taken to visit their home and liked Matilda aunty. She was a very gentle person, a nurse in Sumanti Hospital, which belonged to my friend's father. Rajan, who had not specialized in anything, got some job as administrator in the same place. They used to cook non vegetarian food and she was different from us, in the sense she used lipstick and wore high heeled sandals!

What attracted me to her home was the fact that she used to subscribe to English magazines like 'Woman & Home' and Women's Weekly.' With my craze to read, I would ask her if I could borrow back issues to read the romantic serials! She hardly spoke with me but said I could and so my visits to their home started. Suddenly one day, it was announced that she had died.

There were a lot of whispers as to the cause of her death, and the plight of the poor child, Puttu; none of this really had any impact on me. I only remember thinking that I would not get to read the magazines I used to borrow from her, anymore. Puttu preferred to visit his mother's relatives since he was comfortable with them. I did not really have anything much to do with him. Later on, we became quite friendly and eventually phased out of each other.

I realized around this time that Appa had started drinking. This was also something that I came to know in a strange way. He would invariably be in a very bad mood in the mornings and in the evenings he would go off to the terrace and then it would be Amma's turn to get into a bad mood and Appamma to feel sad. Observing this for some weeks I became curious. One day I went up to the terrace despite strict warnings not to go when he was there. He was so affectionate and soft spoken and asked about my school and studies. Happily I chattered away, till Amma screamed out for me.

But seeing that he was in such a good mood, I would follow him to the terrace every evening and one day mustered up the courage to ask him what he was doing and why was everyone angry with him. He brought out the glass he was hiding and asked if I wanted a sip. I took a small one and went into a fit of coughing. He said it was whisky and since he was very tired after working the whole day he felt relaxed if he had a drink; nobody in the house liked his new drinking habit. I was also hearing rumblings from the others that he had no work and was not earning any money and the only money was from Thatha's salary.

I remember one night, I woke up to some sound and went into my parents' bedroom where I found Appa and Amma fighting. I was so scared, I ran back silently to the hall and into Appamma's arms, who had also heard the sound and woken up. She held me tight, and gently asked me to get into bed beside her. I don't know how long it took for the trembling inside me to subside, but I slept in the comfort of Appamma's arms. The next day she seems to have chastised both Amma and Appa.

After that day I never went up to the terrace to keep Appa company in the evenings. He called me a few times but I just said I was studying. My loyalty was clearly to Amma and I couldn't bear it if anyone made her cry. It became my belief from this point on that if a person needed to smoke or drink hard liquor to boost his or her mood, it was unnatural. At the same time I felt very sorry for Appa. I could see that he was struggling to help Thatha in augmenting the household income and it was not easy. My cup of worries was full because I had to cope with my studies at school all on my own as no one in the family had any knowledge about them.

I don't quite remember how the idea came up but Appa suggested that I go to Rajan uncle's house to study after returning from school since it would be quiet. I started going to my uncle's house and as expected, it was quiet. My uncle came in sometime before I left in the evening with a breezy hi. I was happy because I found that I could achieve progress with my studies. One afternoon, when I went there, my cousin was not to be seen and on asking was told that he had gone out. The cook was pottering around and I was seated in the usual room and soon got engrossed in my Physics lesson.

I was so busy learning up the laws of motion that I did not even hear Rajan uncle coming into the room. All I felt was a pair of arms tightly holding me and when I jumped out of the chair, startled, he simply turned me round to face him and pinning my arms against my back, jammed his face onto mine. I only remember kicking him and then turning and biting whatever came in the range of my teeth – he yelped and his hands loosened and I ran to the door, unlatched it and ran down the stairs all the way home. I was heaving and crying and slumped on Amma's lap. Between sobs I seem to have told her what happened and she soothed me and said I should never have been sent to his house at all. And Appamma said something like 'what else do you expect from a man like him… a widower'

I must have been just 14 years but along 'with the shock of it was a seething anger. 'How dare he…,' I fumed to myself. Amma told Appa and literally badgered him into doing something. Appa called me to go for a drive with him and we went into the adjacent street. He stopped the car and asked what happened. I told him and he said it must have been just a way of showing affection. I said I don't believe he loved me more than Appa and Appa never did anything more than stroke my head gently as a mark of affection. Amma and Appamma would hug me but none of the men in the family used to touch me except for ruffling my head. Then Appa said to me, 'What he did was wrong. I can go and shout at him. But, you see, if I do that he will never be allowed into our house again. All ties will be broken.'

What a burden to put on a 14 year old girl, who did not even fully understand what she had experienced and what it could have resulted in if she had not been able to run for her life the way I did.

Then I understood the power of the family. This feeling of injustice stayed on and still stays on in my mind, that the power of family overpowers everything else. I remembered the incident of the boyi and how differently this very same Appa had behaved. This stayed on in mind for several decades and I was filled with rancor every time I saw my uncle or even remembered what he had done, but at some point of time I just started seeing it as something that is a fact of life.

There were so many happenings all around me at this point of time. Srinu's daughter, Sita, contracted polio and Srinu took her to my doctor, Dr. Chinnana, for treatment. It is remarkable that he was able to cure Sita completely and ensure that she was not crippled by it. When Sita fell sick with polio, Appamma moved into their house because she felt that my aunt Neeraja would find it helpful to have another person assisting in taking care of the child. With all this happening, Thatha suddenly disappeared and did not turn up for months together. There was joy and laughter with Asha's two babies around the place, but I was also filled with a deep sorrow that Thatha was not around.

Those were difficult days. But we did not seem to be poor in that sense. We were simply very careful in our spending. Appa, however, continued his drinking and it was slowly increasing in quantity and he was starting off early and many times did not sit in the office at all. Rajamama meanwhile got a job in Visakhapatnam and moved there. Ammama went to stay with him. I didn't know if she went to keep house for him or she preferred to divide her dependence on her sons by spending some months with each of the three. Generally, the impression I got from the private grumblings and whispered confidences exchanged by women in the family and in the neighborhood was that there was tension between daughters in law and mothers in law in all homes and so the latter kept moving from son to son!

In the midst of all the excitement, confusion, heartache, one day we saw a long haired, bearded man wearing a saffron dhoti, sporting a 'rudrakshamalai[43]' round his neck and clacking wooden sandals standing at the doorstep. I yelped, 'Thatha' and ran to embrace him. Everyone else was very cautious. No questions asked, no explanations given. He said that henceforth he would have only rice and curd for lunch with some pickle. At dinner time he had a glass of milk, sometimes he also ate a banana. He continued his dress code for a few days and then started dressing normally. His diet however, did not change. At the most he would enjoy the luxury of

---

43 Rudrakshmalai – long neck chain made of rudrakshas

fried potatoes with his curd rice. Otherwise it was coffee in the morning, lunch at 1 pm, coffee in the late afternoon and dinner at 8 p.m. The books he read were different – they were Bhavan's Journal, Bhagavad Gita, and Upanishads. So from Keats and Shelley and Alexander Dumas my taste also had to move to the Bhagavad Gita et al. I am truly glad that Thatha did this to me because that is the only way I would have got a grounding in the Hindu religious texts. Nobody else in the family had any such leanings.

Amma performed pujas, celebrated festivals, and inculcated in me a love for classical south Indian music which I also learnt, but this foundation that Thatha laid into my ever absorbent brain I think has been one of the reasons for the core of me remaining untouched. What I learnt from him about the 'atman[44]' and the 'paramatman[45]' played a great role in the way I perceived relationships, friendships, success and disappointment. There was generally a joke that Thatha had gone batty but I think that he probably was the only one who was able to keep himself whole without shattering to bits. He was an amazing man, insofar as his habits were concerned. He was highly disciplined, meticulous, modest about his knowledge and ability, tolerant of his failed sons, and satisfied. He was not infallible and no one is. His younger brothers also had only admiration for him because he sacrificed his studies in order to get a job, earn an income and enable them to pursue their studies. Both of them became famous national figures

In the midst of all this I did not lose my tendency to advocate democratic functioning in school. One incident was that of appointing a head girl – usually this was a girl from

---

[44]   Atman – The soul in Hindu philosophy

[45]   Paramatman – The universal soul or the One, in Hindu philosophy

Class 11 and she was chosen by the Principal. It was always announced that the head girl was elected. I could not, of course, take this lying down. So when I reached Class 11 I questioned the so called election during morning assembly. The Principal looked at me helplessly, the vice principal was shocked and hopping mad and all the senior staff looked askance. I said that if they wished to call it appointment I had no problem but how can it be an election without a contest? The vice principal said it was unanimous and I asked when and how was this decided. Were we asked our opinions? Who does she mean when she says 'unanimous?' If she was alone with me she would simply have hacked me to pieces, I thought. So the topic was adjourned and then we students of Class 11 were asked if anyone would like to contest. Nobody else dared, but just to prove my point I raised my hand.

My opponent was Sanjana Sen. I liked Sanjana a lot and we were quite good friends. I did not go around canvassing but the staff and Sister Mary went around canvassing against me saying that I would come to no good by being defiant and if they wanted to be safe they should not vote for me. Sanjana won and I was so happy that I took her home to meet my family. She came very willingly and was well received by my family. We both always had a close but healthy competition for the first rank.

Given my track record over the span of my entire schooling, I and everyone else expected that I would excel in my Senior Cambridge i.e., school finals also, but it was not to be. I don't know what happened when we went in for our final examinations. I was sure and confident ahead of the examinations, but on the day of our first examination which was Physics Practical, when I entered the examination hall in St. Sebastian High School, my mind went blank and I could not do my experiment. I submitted a blank paper and came out. The same thing happened for the Chemistry and Biology Practicals. Knowing that I had messed up my Practicals I was paralysed during the entire examination and knew that I would fail. I failed and so badly.

Everyone at home was shocked because I was a star performer throughout my schooling. But Appa mockingly said, everyone needs to be knocked down once or twice in order to appreciate the good things in life. So I swallowed the rude blow to my pride and went back to school; in the second attempt, I did well. The unfortunate part of all this was that if I had passed the examination I would have completed Senior Cambridge and that would have certainly given me a kind of thrill. The following year Senior Cambridge was done away with all over India and we had what was called the Indian School Certificate examination only. I rued having missed the chance of having completed my Senior Cambridge.

I finished my ISC examinations and knew I had performed quite well. To be on the safe side I decided to take the Higher Secondary Certificate examination privately from Delhi. I went to Delhi to stay with Thatha's brother for three months. Thatha was also there and Amma accompanied me. A private tutor would come and help me prepare for my examination. In the evenings I used to go cycling in the nearby field with a girl I had befriended in Delhi. Just as the examinations were nearing I had a bad fall from the bicycle and suffered internal injuries on my chest and arm which kept me in bed and I could not take the examination. I returned to Hyderabad disappointed that I had to depend only on the results of the ISC examinations.

Once I returned there was all the preoccupation of what would I do next? My decision was not simple. As it is, I had joined school late and then lost a year by failing in the school finals. I wanted to study medicine but was told by Dr. Chinnana that it was too strenuous for me. My next choice, dairy farming, was vetoed and science subjects were also considered too strenuous so I had no choice but to take up some Arts subject. Appa believed that I needed to study for my graduation in Madras in order to get the necessary cultural education and self-confidence. So Seshumama and Ammama who lived in Madras, were approached and they agreed to be my guardians during my graduate studies.

The move to Madras brought along a lot of changes in my life. I had suddenly become an adult and had to find myself admission in one of the colleges without any support from my family. I could not understand how I became an adult overnight. However the option I faced was to either get myself admission in a graduate college or forego the chance to complete my graduation. I suspected that Appa was himself too nervous to handle the problem of my admission into a college in Madras and simply dumped me.

I secured admission in Lourde Women's College. Thus commenced the golden period of my life. It was fun, learning, friendship, independence, responsibility, leadership. We were all new to each other. Initially, I was a day girl and stayed with Seshumama. His wife Soundarya was pregnant with the second child and was employed in some office. She would leave for work by 9 in the morning. The only memories I have of her are that she was a very loud person and she would rummage through my suitcase and help herself to my favourite cotton saris in exchange for her synthetic saris. I hated synthetic clothing because of the static it produced on my body and I had few but simple, lovely printed saris. There was nothing much I could say since she just helped herself to whatever she pleased. I did resent her casual manner and loud voice but she was also full of jokes and warm in her own way. Her sudden death after childbirth shocked me.

Ammama used to cook and pack me a lunchbox. It was only for me because Seshumama would eat a full meal of rice and leave, so also his wife. In the afternoons he would eat some snack in the canteen and she would go off to her elder sister's house directly. Sometimes the sister would visit us and she always passed some taunting remark when she saw me.

In college we were four classmates who sat together on a stone bench in the college campus at lunch and ate from our respective 'tiffins[46]' the first few days. Then we started sharing our food. Rajam always had a tasty lunch. Mahadevi or Maha, as we called her was a typical curd rice person. I had lime rice as a staple for many weeks. One day I asked Ammama to make something different since I was eating the same thing every day. She gave a tight laugh and started giving me a variety.

Rajam, Maha and I used to board the bus at the Abhiramapuram bus stop in Mylapore and alight at the Santhome beach stop to proceed to college. We all had limited money with us and sometimes we used to walk all the way from the college to our homes in order to save enough money for a 'one by three[47]' cup of coffee at the restaurant in Luz Corner, in Mylapore!

Tragedy struck the family when my aunt Soundarya died 21 days after childbirth. It was the first time I was seeing death at such close quarters and I couldn't believe that a person who was cheerfully talking with me at 5 p.m. would, after 6 hours, be unconscious and then dead. The neighborhood doctor rushed in to examine her and said that she had no chance of living but we could take her to the hospital. She was taken to the hospital and died on the way itself. Everyone was shocked and distraught and totally forgot about the baby. The older

---

[46] Tiffin – lunch box
[47] One by three – one cup divided into three portions

daughter, Srinidhi, could not understand what had happened. I picked up the baby Mukund carefully and tried to feed him with the silver feeder. Somehow the cook and I managed to keep him under control while the funeral arrangements went on. The death took place in Soundarya's mother's house which was just a few houses away from where we lived. The baby and Srinidhi stayed on with their maternal grandmother while Seshumama, Ammama and I returned to our house.

Ammama was in a state of shock and so she was taken away by Amma to our home in Hyderabad. My life suddenly went haywire. Seshumama and I were left in the house. He walked around silently and he had no clue as to what to do in the kitchen. I was expected to cook and I didn't even know how to boil a pan of milk! So it was arranged that I go to his mother in law's house round the corner for my meals. Seshumama would go off to work in the morning ignoring his mother in law's plea to eat something, and it was only late at night that he returned.

The silence and emptiness of the house was eerie. I would sit on the stone bench in the compound initially, but stopped because of the vulgar attentions of some of the men in the colony. I wrote to Appa about this and one fine day, a couple of months later, Thatha landed up at the doorstep; he had a private conversation with Seshumama. The reason for this sudden decision was not so much my letter but the remark Ammama made when Amma expressed to her the difficulties I was having living in Madras without a woman around; Ammama seems to have replied that I was old enough to be married and I should not only be able to manage a home, but also a child, so it was good for me to have some practice, and what is all the fuss about! This angered Amma, who complained to Appa, and Thatha heard the conversation and said that his beloved granddaughter did not go to Madras to cook but to study and that he would take the responsibility for admitting me into the hostel!

Thatha accompanied me to the college where he spoke with the hostel warden about our problem. I got admission into the hostel, Thatha completed all the formalities and bought me all the stuff needed, like bed linen, toiletries, buckets, lunch tray, etc. I was to share a room on the second floor with two more girls. I did not find room sharing a problem since I was in any case used to a kind of community living from childhood. The rush to occupy the bathroom, to secure a good seating in the 'mess,' was all a very familiar experience. My classmates, Mekala, Sharmista, and Rati had rooms at the far end and I enjoyed that we were so close together. Very soon we came to be known as the 'inseparables.' I missed the bus rides and lunch with my day scholar friends and we kept in touch despite my being in the hostel. Our rooms were old, high ceilinged with a tall narrow window and Victorian chest of drawers. We had common toilets and bathing rooms. They were kept clean as well. We had, of course, to clean our rooms and also our clothes. This was something I was not used to. Miss Lucas, the head of the English department who had her little cottage at the far end of the college premises came to know about my predicament, probably from Mekala's conversations. One day her maid turned up at my door and asked me to hand over my clothes to be washed. I was puzzled and Mekala explained that the maid also washed her clothes and 'Lukey' (our nickname for Miss Lucas) must have sensed that I was not used to washing my clothes. She said that I could just pay the maid some money at the end of every month. Very soon 'Thai[48]' also started cleaning my room.

---

[48]   Thai – meaning mother and term used in Madras in those days to refer to house helps

From the verandah of our block we could get a view of the marvelous sea and it was lovely to sleep to the sounds of the sea waves every night. After a few weeks one girl was shifted to another room so we were only two girls and that was comfortable. Mekala, Rati, Sharmista and I became very close friends and we used to call ourselves the 'Four Musketeers.' For a short period, Ruth joined our gang but moved out of the group just as quietly as she came in. We had a table at the mess which none other dared to occupy. All of these perks were due to the fact that Mekala was a Malyali and the entire lot of cooks and servers were Malyalis. Only the cleaners were Tamil.

The food in the mess was awful but Mekala had a cousin with whose help she used to smuggle in food from outside and so we were quite well fed! We were the stars of our class and had a real interest in English literature. We used to meet on the terrace every fortnight after everyone went to sleep and with the help of candles and torches we would read poetry. We fixed in advance which poet we would focus on for the month – so we had a Wordsworth month, a Shelley month and so on. Madras, at this time, was going through a major political transition. The DMK[49] party was gathering up its strength as a new opposition to the Congress. One manifestation was the rise and strengthening of trade unions all over Tamilnadu and the other was a strong focus on reservation for Scheduled Castes (SCs) in educational institutions.

Our college had a high quota for SCs. I had not thought much about caste and exclusion and generally was rather naïve in thinking that SCs were dark and poor and sweaty. This kind of identification had no meaning in Tamilnadu because mostly people were dark skinned and the climate was such

---

[49] DMK – Dravida Munnetra Kazhagam, a Tamilnadu based political party

that everyone was sweaty. What struck me as amazing was the fact that in the hostel mess, the servers could identify SCs in a jiffy and would always serve them last, and ladle out the food from a height so they did not touch the 'untouchable'. The servers whom we called 'mess boys' were a jolly lot and always came with much laughter and cheer to serve us, but just a few tables away, in the very same dining hall, we would hear their voices changing into one of harsh rudeness. We would always anticipate for that harshness to erupt. I feel ashamed at my denseness and ignorance every time I recall these incidents.

Once I asked 'Lukey' why these girls were treated in such a manner in the mess. She replied that since they were on scholarships, they got free meals and that is why the mess boys behaved in that manner, assuming that they were doling out the food. We were not convinced by this explanation; while the other three of our gang dismissed the matter, Ruth and I did not and dug a little further, befriending the girls. Initially, the girls were very cautious thinking we were going to cause them problems but reassured that we were above board, a couple of them opened up; one of them said that they were 'untouchables' and were therefore accommodated in the worst rooms on one floor with hardly any natural lighting and allotted triple sharing rooms. They were discriminated against in every aspect from food to accommodation to healthcare because of their caste. They spoke about being exploited in many other ways. Being as dense as possible, I asked like what and the girl who was just about 17 laughed and said 'see, you don't even know what the facts of life are. We are your age or younger than you and we know.'

I remember talking about this to Chinnathatha when I visited him. I just talked about what was happening in the hostel and dismissed it from my mind. But later, I was called by the college Principal / hostel Warden and she said 'so you are the communist...' and I was quite puzzled as to what she meant. Then 'Lukey' asked how I could dare to send information to the Bombay newspaper. I denied having done anything of the sort but she would not believe me. She became quite cold towards me and stopped sending 'thayi' for my clothes. She also believed that I was responsible for some newspaper article that I have not seen to date!

Shortly thereafter I was down with an attack of paratyphoid and once the diagnosis was made, I had to be moved out of the sick room. I preferred going to a hospital rather than to Seshumama's house. I was admitted in the general ward in Kalyani Government Hospital. For the first week I was delirious with fever and not allowed any visitors from college. The recovery was slow and when the hostel matron said she would intimate my parents I asked her not to and that I would tell her when to do so.

Once I started recovering, I wrote a few lines about my illness on a postcard to Amma. Appa sent a telegram congratulating me on my courage and determination. I was started off on solid food and it would be cold idli with a small hot stainless steel glass of coffee, lunch was thick grains of rice with sambar. I managed the breakfast but it was impossible to get down even a morsel of the rice served for lunch. The doctor was a very lovely person and she would come and try to feed me some mouthfuls. On days she did not come I would simply hand over my plate of food to my neighbouring patient since she was able to polish off her helping as well as mine.

When I was discharged and taken to the hostel, I was so fragile and weak, a light whiff of breeze could have blown me off. I had to climb up two flights of steps and wondered how I would manage that. My gang of four just carried me up and laid me on my bed. This experience is something I can never forget till I die. We all cried together at my plight. Then we cried some more out of joy that we were all together and I was alive. Only then did I realize how close I had been to dying.

There was so much else going on around us. It was 1965, when the country was going through difficult times with the government at the Centre experiencing political simmering and threats on the Indo China border. We followed the prime minister's call to miss a meal and on one day of the week the entire hostel had some kind of watery payasam[50]. It was a thrill to have to blacken our windows with newspaper and practice a mock drill of running to the garden and hiding behind the bushes when the alarm went off!

Our college meanwhile had its own share of 'political simmering.' The daughters of two political honchos were studying in our college. They were always together. One of them was calm and friendly but the other was intolerant of us. Both of them used to have special lunch served to them from our mess in the Principal's room. When our gang came to know of this we objected and told the deputy warden that the girls should eat what we ate and where we ate. Thinking back now, I wonder why we were so sanctimonious!

We completed our first year examinations and went into second year where the studies got tougher. In mid-1966, in Tamilnadu, the DMK swept into power breaking the age old Congress regime. In February 1967, at lunch time, one of the girls found a praying mantis in her sambar and screamed in horror. We all rushed and when we saw what it was we refused to eat. The five of us organized a lightning strike and all the hostel students refused to eat. We stood in the mess clanging our spoons against our plates.

---

50   Payasam – a porridge like dessert made with lentils and jaggery

The deputy warden came and tried to bully us and then calm us down but we were really mad. We went to our classes after a half hour and none of us had any lunch. Around 7 in the evening, the Principal / Warden came with two huge baskets of oranges. We had been summoned to the mess and she looked around and asked who started the protest. Nobody uttered a sound. She curtly told us to go and take an orange each and behave ourselves. Nobody moved. She gave one warning, two and then said this is my last and final warning. Nobody stirred. It was past 9 p.m. and she was tired with our determination. That was my first lesson in how to effectively protest. Silently persist in your protest and the confronted party gets worn out.

Without realizing it we came to know that for the first time in the history of any women's college in Tamilnadu and definitely the history of Lourde Women's College, an incorrigible group of 5 as we were known, had staged a lightning strike and succeeded. The fact that this hardly got noticed is indicative of the importance given to women and girls in those days. There was no media coverage. Seshumama, when he heard the whole story from me, laughed and said 'you girls actually had a successful lightning strike – I can't believe it!' We realized that once you start something like a strike, you can't just end it and very soon we had taken on more than we could chew.

The college elections were slated to take place and we stalled it. The hostel students insisted that a mess committee be formed which will look into the functioning of the mess right from purchase to stores to the billing section – and the first committee comprised of the five of us. It was a painful, but truly amazing revelation to the five of us as to how corruption is intertwined at every step. The morning milk was being diluted for us and good milk sold out by the milkman from which he gave a cut to the chief cook of our mess. The same pattern was repeated in the case of vegetables, groceries, etc. And finally the bill that was being prepared for us to pay at month end was also being inflated.

As Mess Committee members, each of us had to maintain a minutes' book wherein our daily tasks and observations were minuted, signed by us and cosigned by the deputy warden. We worried at what we had taken on and the fact that our 1st year examinations were fast approaching. From being star students in our classes we were being reprimanded for late entry into class, incomplete home assignments and sudden disappearance from class. Our studies were badly affected because we had taken on the responsibility of running a mess committee. I was hostel secretary.

We would be called in the middle of a class or just before commencement of one, for some meeting or for checking the arrival of some grocery or cross checking some accounts. We didn't know how to handle the situation. On one occasion, Rati was checking the kitchen and there was some altercation between her and the chief cook. The chief cook seemed to have had an arrangement with the supplier of groceries, vegetables and milk and got substandard stuff with fraudulent bills. This bill was the basis on which the mess charges were levied on us hostellers. With us in charge, he was obviously deprived of a sizeable chunk of side income on a monthly basis. This income when we calculated, would have been more than his actual salary. His resentment was creating problems. The problems spiraled into a serious issue because Rati was Bengali and the cook was Malyali with very limited understanding of English. She seemed to have pulled him up for the substandard groceries. She had a loud and commanding voice but she was never abusive in either her language or treatment of anybody.

The chief cook complained to the deputy warden that Rati had spoken to him in abusive language and she summoned us for a meeting. Rati explained what had taken place and said that if he felt slighted, she was sorry for it. The meeting was recorded in the minutes book and one sentence read something like, "Rati Bose apologized to Madhavan Nair for her misbehavior with him on … date." The five of us signed below and so did the deputy warden. I then took the minutes books because I usually kept them in my custody. We dismissed this incident since our focus was totally on preparation for the fast approaching examinations.

Sharmista and Rati had French as special language, Mekala and I had taken Hindi. The Hindi syllabus was quite high, with grammar, history of Hindi literature, prose and poetry. I was quite good at languages and had been able to keep pace despite the disturbances. But for Mekala it was tough. I promised to help her during the examinations. We studied through the night. We used to buy idlis from the canteen in the afternoon and store them in our rooms. We got together around 9 p.m. on the stairs leading to the terrace. The five of us would sit studying till 3 or 4 a.m. every day. We started feeling hungry around midnight and we would eat the idlis with pickle which Sharmista had a supply of. We did not realize what a shock we were in for on the eve of our examinations.

When the hall tickets were being given, we found that our four names were missing from the list. We asked what happened and were told to go and meet the Principal. We went and she made us wait outside the office for around two hours. Then she called us in and said that if we thought we were smart she would 'show us.' She said she was withholding our hall tickets because we had misbehaved. We were frantic.

I managed to send information to Seshumama asking him to telephone me urgently. He came to see me and I took him into the garden and explained what was happening. He asked me to give the names of the four of us. I had written them already and holding his hand casually, placed the slip of paper in his palm. He said not to worry, but the examinations were just four days away and we were breaking with tension. What would we tell our parents?

We had just about entered adulthood and each of us had a boyfriend somewhere in the country. It was rather strange that Mekala, Rati and I had boyfriends who were in the armed forces. Our boyfriends were all on the Indo China border. Sharmista had a fiancée approved by her family. I did not have any plans of marriage but the other three were all set to tie the knot right after graduation. And here we were, just nearing the end of 2nd year, in neck deep trouble.

The next day, around noon we got a summons from the Principal. When we entered she said that we might have used political influence this time and she was releasing our hall tickets, but she would show us not to play around with her. Barely understanding her we rushed off to collect the hall tickets from the office before she changed her mind. The counter clerk looked at us with awe and said 'Aiyyo[51], you have so much influence…the education minister himself telephoned and told her to release your hall tickets.' I was impressed with Seshumama's influence. It also taught me the crucial role people's movements and trade unions play in the growth and strengthening of new political parties. He later telephoned and asked me to wrap the minutes books in newspaper and hand them over to him at the college gate I did so. The examinations started and we were busy.

On the day of the last examination the Principal called me and Rati and asked us to hand over the minutes books to her. We nodded and left. We ran out and once the four of us

---

[51]   Aiyyo – an exclamation akin to 'Oh my'

got together we wondered what could be the reason for her wanting the minutes books and how Seshumama zeroed in on what she had planned to use against us. I came to know the reason when I went to his house once college vacations commenced. He took out the books and leafed through Rati's minutes' book till he came to the page of the misbehavior with the chief cook. That, he said, was what she planned to use against us.

I was puzzled and he said the connotations of 'misbehavior' were vast and there was no detail as to exactly what transpired. So she could, with the connivance of the deputy warden and the chief cook accuse Rati of anything and considering that he was an employee and she a student from an economically privileged family, the implications could be serious. What shall we do? I asked, and he gave one of his rare mischievous laughs. We went to the backyard. He just dumped all the books into the well!

I don't know when I slipped into adulthood but it just happened. It was probably the Chinese aggression and the fact that Shekhar my boyfriend who was in the Indian Air Force was on the border. We had met when I was in Delhi preparing for my Higher Secondary examinations and it was a lovely friendship where he used to tease me till I cried and then he would apologise with the funniest antics he could think of to set me laughing! He subsequently came to the Airforce Academy in Hyderabad and we kept our friendship going. When I went to Madras he would write me long letters most of which just had the sentence 'I love you so very very much' repeated over and over again! Once he got his border posting, his letters became erratic and the address to which I could write was always c/o of P.O. No. I would never know if he received my letters till I got a letter from him confirming that he had. There was very little he could write and so it was just a few lines asking how I was and asking me to wait for him because he wanted to marry me! He did not find it necessary to ask me if I wanted to marry him...

It was at this point of time that I realized how much time I had wasted mindlessly arguing with him and fighting and going into silent sulks when we did have the opportunity to build a relationship during his visits to our Hyderabad home. He would come only to meet me while the pretext was that of reporting to my parents who were his local guardians. He used to joke and try to make me laugh but never succeeded. He seriously tried asking me what the matter was, and nothing really, was the matter, except that I seem to have been too mixed up about my own feelings, where I would invite my closest friend Renu home on his visits and then feel jealous when he laughed and talked with her in a manner bordering on flirtation!

Before we knew it, I had to leave for Madras for my graduate studies and we never got to meet again. The realization of the importance of saying what one has in mind at the right time and understanding that time only moves forward, never back, was one sign I saw as my entry into adulthood. I wished then that I had another chance but life was already written out for me and all I could do was move with the tide. The Indo Pakistan war followed and that was the end of my contact with my boyfriend. No letters came and when, with the help of Rati's fiancé, I did try to trace him, the news was that he was among the missing POWs[52]. In a fit of rage at myself and deep sorrow, one day, I took all his letters to the backyard of the hostel and set fire to them.

We all went to our respective homes, presumably for the end of the academic year break. My sister Asha had a male

---

[52] POW –Prisoner of War

child in January. This child, Kiran, was almost like my son. I loved him and he loved me too. I fed him his meals, bathed and dressed him, and he even insisted on sleeping beside me. By the time I returned home for the vacation, Appa had rented out the ground floor of our new house and we lived on the first floor. I could not have the independent room with a proper cot and bed I had enjoyed when we first shifted to our new home. The luxury, after so many years of sleeping on a straw mat was lost. I did not however resent the loss.

My carefree attitude to life was soon crushed by the entry of a lecherous uncle into my life. He would walk into the room late in the evening where Asha was on the floor feeding Kiran and casually sit on the cot where I was lying with a sheet covering me; he would then daringly slip his hand inside my nightshirt and crush my breasts while carrying on a conversation with her. I was too shocked and paralysed. I kept pushing him and would go and sit beside Asha on the floor. He would daringly come and sit beside me and slip his hand again. This happened on two of his visits.

From the next time on, whenever he came I would shut myself in the lavatory and he was so persistent, I had to once remain in the lavatory for over 40 minutes. But I knew there was no point in complaining to anybody because either nobody believed he could behave like that or nobody wanted to confront him. I had to fend for myself. This realization was the second sign that I was now an adult and so, many of the uncomfortable problems I had to sort out for myself. I would say from 18 years onwards many girls and boys become what I call 'young adults.' I became a young adult slightly later than other girls because of various reasons, mainly the fact that I had such an illness ridden childhood. Coming back to the menace of this male relative who I saw as the sex ogre in my life, I thought it was only a summer vacation at the end of which I could go back to my hostel and thereafter see that I did not have to come back to my parents' house at all and not have to manage his obnoxious behavior. But fate had it otherwise. What drove him to behave the way he did, as long as he was alive is something I cannot comprehend.

One day, Appa came and said that he knew I would not come to any good in life and I had proved it. 'What?!' I asked and he waved a letter at me. I took it and saw it was from the Principal of Lourde Women's College. She said that I could not get admission into the hostel for the next semester on, since I was an antisocial element and my presence would be a bad influence on the rest of the students. I got letters from the other three friends within the week that they had got similar letters. In the case of Mekala, 'Lukey' stood guarantee. Sharmista's mother gave an undertaking that her daughter would not maintain her friendship with us and she was also allowed into the hostel. So Rati and I were the only ones affected. Rati was applying to the Residency Hostel for accommodation and would continue her studies but Appa was not prepared to send me to Residency Hostel. He also felt that I had not done anything wrong and there was no assurance that even if he did give an apology on my behalf, the Principal would not mess up my conduct certificate or refrain from putting a spoke in my studies thereafter.

It was such a complicated state of affairs, because I had performed exceedingly well in my last semester in all the subjects including Hindi. The subject grouping in Hyderabad was different from Madras and I did not know how I would get admission into a college in such a situation. Asha came to my rescue. Since she was teaching in a women's college for so many years and was a favourite of not only the

Principal but was also respected by the management, she stated my problem to the Principal and secured a seat for me in Kamma College with the grouping of English Literature, Economics and Political Science. She gave strict instructions that I should not take advantage of our relationship, should not tell any of the students I befriended that we were related and that at all times before contemplating any mischief I should remember that she was my sister and her reputation was at stake.

I promised to behave. The good part was that I would be admitted into the second year and I should complete my first year examinations alongside the second year examinations and if I failed I would be moved back to first year. It was so much more slogging but I did not grudge it because I didn't think I would graduate at all when I got thrown out of Lourde Women's College.

The phase in Kamma College was yet another interesting chapter in my very adventurous life! The silver lining was that I renewed my friendship with Mahrukh and that was a steady factor in my life at that point, because she was mature and practical, doing what she felt was best for her. The drudge started with my having to run to the bus stop every morning from Penny Nursing Home to the city bus terminus and then boarding a bus to Bimalguda, alighting at the crossroads and walking to the college. Since I was living at home, it was possible for me to have a greater variety of saris what with Amma's collection also being available. She also wore cotton saris with small light colored print and always kept the best ones aside for me to select what pleased me. She always kept a string of fresh jasmines for my plait every day. The most attractive features in me I was told, were my thick, long plait swinging side to side as I walked and my large eyes. Otherwise

I was a thin, mingy creature, with practically a single thick eyebrow and long nose.

It was very interesting for me to note that most of the college girls, even if walking to the bus stop in a group or in pairs, would never sit together in the bus. Each would sit by a window and giggle and later a boy would gauchely go and sit beside one of them. I liked sitting by the window because my thoughts could fly with the breeze. One day, a lanky boy with the hint of a moustache came and sat beside me. I promptly told him it was a 'ladies' seat and he should move. He looked a bit surprised but moved away quietly.

During my graduate studies I had two sets of friends – one set was introduced to me by a faculty, stating that this was the kind of group I should move around with. They were two girls, very gentle, very 'good' and studious. The other set comprised of girls who befriended me on their own and were a loud, laughter loving sort. I maintained my friendship with both sets and so won the hearts of the faculty and also had my share of college fun. The English and Hindi syllabus were a cakewalk for me since I had a much tougher syllabus in my previous college. There were two new subjects I had to get the hang of – one was Economics and the other was Political Science. It did not take me very long to do so and I was a free bird to go loafing with the fun-loving, carefree gang of friends.

The carefree gang was one which believed in seeing the first screening of any Hindi movie that was released. There were almost 10 movie halls near about our college and one of the girls would be entrusted with the task of buying the tickets. At the end of the movie we would settle payments for the movie ticket, any snacks we may have had, shared rickshaws, etc. These settlements were very clear and none of us tried to cheat the others. There was one hidden agenda the girls had that I never knew about and this was 'boyfriend hunting;' there were a set of boys who were interested in one or other of the girls in our gang and this movie outing was a pretext for the girl and boy to see each other. When I came to know of this I asked them not to involve me in any of their games and promised not to squeal on them even inadvertently. Thankfully, all of us kept up to our promises and life went on smoothly.

I looked forward to visiting Mahrukh on the odd Sunday when I would share these juicy bits of gossip. She had graduated in Commerce and got a job as a clerk in Midland Bank, on Bankers Street in Hyderabad. She would laughingly ask why I did not get myself a boyfriend. I just brushed it off saying I did not have the time. One such Sunday, she was going to the hairdressers round the corner and I accompanied her. While preparing Mahrukh for a hair trim, the hairdresser asked if I would like to trim the split ends in my hair. And I said yes – when she asked me what length she should trim off – I said I wanted a style like Mahrukh's. She looked wide eyed and asked 'are you sure?' and I said of course and Mahrukh said, 'Usha, think it over,' I said 'No, I want a haircut.'

I was made to sit on a high chair, a tunic draped on me and the woman started chopping my hair. As I saw the thick tresses falling to the floor, I burst into tears. Mahrukh came and held me and crooned it was alright and it would grow back in no time. I looked awful, but what was done could not be undone. I went home. Appa saw me and said 'See what's come home… a shorn cat.' Nobody said anything. It must have been that they could sense my own dismay and shock at my appearance. It was not common or accepted for a young woman of my age to sport a short hairstyle. A long plait was swinging at the hips was such a pride for girls in the 1960s. The only thing Amma did that evening was to tell the flower seller in a loud voice, not to bring flowers in the evening anymore.

That night I kept searching for my plait to hold between my fingers, a habit I had acquired many years ago. I cried myself to sleep at my self-imposed loss. The next morning, patting my hair in place and bracing myself for the day ahead I went off to the bus stand; there were so many stares, I couldn't believe my eyes. It seemed like the entire public at the bus terminus was staring at me. By the time I reached college there were more stares. Around 7 that evening there was a phone call for me. Rather unusual, I thought. It was from one of my 'gang.' She laughed and asked, 'So you're looking very smart'. I asked how she knew and she said that her brother's friend told him and he in turn told her. I wondered who it was. She then said that it was the same boy who had once tried to sit beside me on the bus and whom I had pushed out. She went on to tell me as to how much he loved me and could not stop thinking about me and so on. I asked her to tell the boy that I was not and never would be interested in him and also told her that I did not want to continue my friendship with her gang anymore because I did not approve of what they were up to. So that ended my friendship with that gang and my concentration was fully on my studies.

As time passed, I managed to let my hair grow long enough, though it never grew to the length it originally was. I completed my 1st year examinations with flying colours and also my second year examinations. I remember getting around A++ grades in Hindi and Economics. They were public examinations so it meant that I was among the toppers at the city level 2nd year degree. I was very happy. The college awarded me the gold medal for excellence in English and the rolling shield for excellence in Economics. One set of the teaching faculty wanted me to be awarded the best all-rounder rolling shield and the other, led by my sister, felt it inappropriate. My friend Durdana got it. She deserved it.

My sister confessed to me later that she led the decision not to award me the all-rounder shield and I said it was fine since I was in any case not an all-rounder because I did not participate in any sports activity. She seemed relieved because she thought I would probably resent her for it. Had she but known that I did have a head on my shoulders! For me, she and Rajamama were the ideal couple and their family the unique one. I did not show it but I worshipped the ground she walked on. Maybe she never realized it. At home I did not expect any praise for my performance and did not get it either. Rajamama, however, was very happy for me and gave me a hug. Mahrukh was ever so happy when she came to know of my success.

Life went on as usual. It was rather strange that the ever so strong friendship that we four musketeers in Lourde Women's College Madras shared, just blew away. We were all so busy with our lives. I heard that Rati married her 'commander' boyfriend just as she completed her final year examinations. Sharmista and Mekala got married within a year. I remember that on one of those unforgettable nights when we had our midnight poetry sessions, we had vowed that five years after graduation we would all meet in the same college and go to the same terrace. I remembered, but don't know if the others did. In any case, I could do nothing about it since I didn't have any money to travel to Madras or even buy postage to write letters to my friends. And so yet another circle of friendship had gone up in smoke.

When I reached final year in Kamma College, the Telengana agitation started in Hyderabad and neighbouring districts. Educational institutions shut down indefinitely. I felt cursed that my studies had to go through such rough weather but tried to make the best of it. There was a small typewriting institute on the main road not far from home. So I went there and started learning typewriting and shorthand.

Thatha promptly ordered a set of Pitman's Shorthand Manual and Guide. It was a great asset in those days. The instructor in the institute asked me to bring it to the institute but I never took it because I did not trust him to not snatch it from me. I practised at home and soon mastered my speed and strokes. That was my shorthand and typing phase. I remember that every spoken or written word I would mentally convert to strokes and dots and dashes!

All of us were having a rough time at home. Appa had become an alcoholic and over some years, not attending to his clients' cases at all. He was abusing Amma so badly; I would get really mad at him and try my best to hide his liquor but he somehow managed to get his hands on it. The previous year Amma had tried to end her life. I'll never forget that scene: one evening, as I walked back home from the bus stop after college, I saw my younger brother Srikar standing near the gate crying and Appa was beside him, drunk, with a stupid grin on his face. As I ran across the street he said 'Your mother swallowed Gamaxene'.[53] I rushed to what was Thatha's room and found her lying on the cot with a tube hanging from her mouth. The person who had rendered the first aid said that most of the pesticide had been flushed out and she was out of danger. My sister Asha living next door also rushed in and we initially wondered if Amma needed to get into a hospital. We decided against it as it would unnecessarily become a medico legal case. I sat beside her while Asha went to console Srikar. Kavi my elder brother landed up in the evening and after some discussion we felt that it was best for Amma to get out of the environment for some time. At first she resisted but agreed on our insistence. She said she would like to go to Agra where her sister was living. So we got her a ticket and she left. It was amazing that without

---

[53]   Gamaxene – pesticide used in homes to ward off cockroaches

any companion, after an attempt at suicide she quite calmly boarded the train to Agra – she did all this without informing her sister that she was visiting her. This convinced us that she had recovered and I realized how disastrous it would be for us to lose her. I knew that she would not attempt something like that ever again. The desperation with Appa's behavior had momentarily clouded her thinking as a result of which she had forgotten our existence and our need for her love and strength.

Having got her out of the way I tried to get Appa to stop drinking. I remember that the final examinations of my graduate studies were looming round the corner and yet I felt the need to take on this responsibility. At first I was so angry I slapped him, but relented when he just stood there taking the beating silently meekly cowering. Crying bitterly, I slowly led him to the bed and made him lie down. I then took away his bottle and emptied the contents. Once he got out of his stupor he started growling for his liquor. I said I had thrown it out and if he wanted us to stay in the house he had to stop drinking. He looked at me and asked timidly if he could have some food. I mixed some soft rice and rasam[54] and fed him. He lay down again and asked for some tranquillizer. I gave him a Calmpose and he went off to sleep. Though I hated Appa's drinking and felt betrayed by him in many ways, I had an unconditional love for him.

I was absorbed in my preparation for my examinations, only taking a break for a short nap. It must have been around 11 in the night one day and Appa came to me, asking if he could please have a small drink. I screamed at him to leave me in peace; I was so loud that everyone at home and even at Asha's house woke up and came rushing. I was shouting and crying and hitting him asking if he wanted all of us to die

---

[54]   Rasam – light soup made of tomatoes, tamarind and mild spices

or what. He then cried and said that he would stop drinking but to please help him because he couldn't sleep and had nightmares. I said I couldn't care less since we were all having nightmares because of him. From the next day on he changed, and became very sober. With my hectic study schedule on one side, I would keep a hawk's eye on his movements. His sudden sober and quiet behavior troubled me and out of suspicion that he was drinking, I would do crazy things like climbing onto the overhead water tanks to see if he had hidden any bottles. I would shake out all his clothes in the cupboard, search behind his law books. It was unbelievable that he had just given up drinking so suddenly, and I was filled with suspicion as to how he just gave up the habit so easily. There was something amiss, but I could not spot it due to my preoccupation with my studies.

He used to behave in the most bizarre manner possible to get even with me. I remember that I used his huge and beautiful teak writing table in his office room for my studies. My books were randomly strewn across the table as I was getting set to prepare for my Political Science examination. I had been reading nonstop from around 8 pm till 3 a.m. and then I retired for a short rest. After waking up at 4 a.m., I resumed my reading and only much later in the evening noticed that three of my books were missing. It puzzled me and I searched the whole house. Finally, I gave up and managed to study with what books I had. A whole year later, when Amma and I were spring-cleaning the house I found the books at the bottom of an empty cardboard carton on the loft of Appa's office room. When I asked him he blandly said that he wanted me to fail in my examinations! He wanted to teach me a lesson that I should not try to set right his life. I was duly repaid for the uphill task I had taken of keeping Appa off liquor!

One morning, just before my examinations were to commence I found Amma on the doorstep – she had returned from Agra. We brought her bags in and I hugged her, asking how come she returned and she said, but you wanted me back. I was still puzzled and she then produced a telegram from her bag which had my name as sender and asking her to please come or I can't write my examination. Appa was standing behind me with a stupid grin on his face and I realized he had sent it. She quietly walked away, avoiding his gaze and settled herself down. She got down to taking care of the house, literally spooning food into my mouth while I kept poring over a book. I finished my examinations and knew I had done well despite all the tension at home. Appa was of course, very quiet and gentle and my only observation was that he would invariably mellow down by around 7 or 8 in the evening. I told my sister Asha this and she said it couldn't be that he was drinking again, because we were watching him all the time so where would he hide the liquor... we thought he had really kicked the drinking habit. One evening, he laughed at us and said 'You thought you were smart but I'm your father remember that...'

For almost two months he had actually been hiding the liquor in empty Horlicks bottles, behind the rice and flour bins on the loft of the dining room. He showed us how, and Asha and I simply burst out laughing. This is when I realized he was an alcoholic. It was not shattering but the question was as to how we dealt with the problem. From then on, when his clients telephoned I would simply say, 'my father is an alcoholic and if he has taken court fees from you and not filed your case there is nothing we at home can do about it'. Appa tried to bully me but I was unfazed. He behaved most abominably and treated Amma very badly. I was not aware of what exactly he did for a very long time because she never revealed anything to me. He found the total indifference from all of us quite unbearable but there was nothing we could do. We were all tired and it was too much for us to take charge of our lives and also care for him.

Every festival he would get into a bout of drinking. We had been celebrating all our festivals with such fun and gaiety right from as far back into my childhood as I can remember. This continued and Amma never thought of just dropping the celebration because of Appa's drinking bouts. I particularly remember that during Navarathri, when we had the 'bommaikoluvu[55]', and invited ladies from the neighbourhood and also other family friends living in the city for 'vethalepakku[56]' there would be an air of tension. If Appa was on a drinking spree we would be so afraid that he might swagger into the room and shock the visitors. What was Amma trying to do, I would wonder then – maintain her own sense of equilibrium or try to make us feel we were in a normal situation or prove to our society that everything was fine within our family? The same festivals that we so enjoyed and looked forward to during childhood, I started dreading and detesting as I grew older. The tension was so high and the pretense so unnecessary. But all through, Amma did not give up.

I realize now that it must have been important for her to maintain her sanity and feeling of family togetherness as well as community acceptance. Later on in life, I recognized the importance of celebration and from the time I started living alone, even to this day, I celebrate every festival. Just

---

[55] Bommaikoluvu – arrangement of idols and handicraft dolls during the 9 days of Navarathri or Dasera

[56] Vethalepakku – betel leaves and areca nut given to guests / visitors at functions

as Amma used to I also maintain a 'puja'[57] space. There is a fairly ornate pedestal with idols of various gods and goddesses neatly arranged. I light the lamps and two incense sticks every morning. It provides a kind of connection for me and gives a sense of fulfilment and peace. The celebration of festivals revives my happier memories during times when Appa had not turned alchoholic and the sense of togetherness we enjoyed. The memories of preparation for the festivals are unforgettable and everything was filled with a sense of purpose right from shopping to decorating the house. I recall Krishnashtami, and the seriousness with which we decorated the floor at every doorstep from the main entrance to the shrine where Krishna's idol was kept with 'kolam' of small feet, symbolizing infant Krishna's feet; our making sweet and salt cheedai[58] as offering to infant Krishna; the special dinner on Krishnashtami. Shopping for the right Vinayaka and all the other specific puja items for Vinayaka Chaturthi is still fascinating and I remember the excitement with which we ate lunch out of lotus leaves on Vinayaka Chathurthi festival, and how we clapped our hands with glee when Amma poured hot rasam onto the central part of the leaf from where it bubbled over; I remember Appamma used to commission a carpenter to set up the nine tiered stage for the Bommaikoluvu or 'Golu' as it is commonly referred to by Tamilians; the concentration with which I would decorate the floor at the bottom of the step with the 'hridayakamalam kolam[59] every day because Amma said that unmarried girls who draw it perfectly get the husband of

---

[57] Puja - worship
[58] Cheedai —crispies made from a dough consisting of rice flour, sesame seeds, oil and a lot of butter particularly for Krishnashtami
[59] Hriydayakamalam - lotus of the heart

their dreams, is funny but reminiscent of the 'normal girly' dreams I had!

I remember being given the task of setting up vethalaipakku onto trays. It consisted of 4 betel leaves, two areca nuts, two sticks of turmeric and one banana (for girls) or one coconut(for women); the heavenly fragrance of sandalwood paste and bitter tinged samanti [60]flowers wafting across the room hits my nose even to this day; there would be crowds of women dressed in their best Kanjeevaram silk saris who started coming in groups from 4 p.m. onwards for nine days; we would visit other people's homes in a similar manner; the Saraswati puja was on day 8 when we would place our books at the feet of Goddess Saraswati; the festival would end with the Ayudha Puja when we placed screwdrivers, wrenches, hammers and the like for the puja and also performed a puja for our cute, blue Simca.

This festival was closely followed by Deepavali where the preparation of sweets and other snacks started days ahead, new dresses were tailored or bought for everyone in the house from the worker to the master, earthen lamps were purchased, along with wicks and oil for use on the festival, as were crackers of all kinds. The festival dawned early in the morning with each of us having to go through the ritual of oil being smeared all over our head and body followed by the Gangasnanam[61].

I found it curious that the importance of Navarathri in our house was to ensure that the blessings of Goddess Saraswati would always be on our head. Deepavali was the celebration of Rama's return from his long exile and successful destruction of Ravana. We never considered it as a celebration of Lakshmi the goddess of wealth. It was always taught to us that knowledge is wealth and right always triumphs over wrong. I must admit

---

[60]   Samanti - chrysanthemums

[61]   Gangasnanam – bath with water from the holy river Ganges

that I felt superior to my other non-Brahmin Hindu friends who worshipped Durga and Lakshmi. Whatever be the belief, we cherished the lovely food we had, the crackers, the beautiful sight of all the houses down the street lit with the steady glow of earthen lamps at night fall. Karthigai Pournami was yet another festival of lights when 'laddus[62]' of jaggery, peanuts and sesame were made and offered in the evening puja and once again the earthen lamps would light up the compound walls of our homes.

Closely following Karthigai was the Margazhi[63] masam when Amma would bathe early every morning and sing the Tirupavvai while going about her chores. We would decorate the entrance of our homes with 'kolam' and place a ball of dung with a flower perched atop in its centre. We did this every day for around 24 days, I think. We would collect the previous day's dried dung ball and store in the kitchen. The day before the commencement of the Pongal[64] festival we kids would go with Appa and buy kites, tall sugarcane sticks, turmeric saplings with roots intact, all varieties of vegetables, pumpkins, coconuts; on the festival day, while massive cooking was going on we kids used to go up to the terrace and fly the kites. This was essentially a boys' sport but Kavi gamely allowed me also to hold the kite for some time. On Pongal day food consisting of a lot of rice and coconut dishes was cooked with the cowdung balls we had stored over the entire month. A lot of food was cooked so that visitors could also partake of the meal. I remember one year when 4 members of the P.T. Iyengar family living on the street at the back of ours came visiting and Appamma served all of them lunch. They were all hearty

---

[62] Laddus – rounded lumps
[63] Margazhi - The last month in the Tamil calendar
[64] Pongal – harvest festival heralding the new year in Tamilnadu

eaters and after they left we had to cook afresh since we ran out of food!

Appamma used to make the preparations the previous evening for the third day or 'kanumu pongal'; she and Amma would make three portions of the left over white rice and one of the portions would be mixed with turmeric powder while another portion would be mixed with the 'kumkum[65]' powder. The third portion would remain white and a portion of the 'chakkarepongal[66]' would also be kept with the three mounds of rice. Incense sticks, and a small earthern lamp would be readied with oil and a cotton wick. The rice powder for the 'kolam' would also be kept along with four turmeric leaves.

On Kanumu Pongal day we women and girls used to go up to the terrace early in the morning and place turmeric leaves on a cleaned surface decorated with 'kolam' and then take two balls of colored rice in our hands and say to ourselves, one for the crow and one for the sparrow, may they always live in harmony. This was so that we as family stayed together and brothers and sisters kept the bonding. As long as Kavi was dependent he was made to hand over some gift to Asha and me, but once he started earning, he would give me a sari for Pongal without fail.

All of this was so full of meaning, bonded us so beautifully and enriched our lives, so probably that is what Amma wanted us not to lose faith in. The size of each festival diminished year on year but the celebration never stopped. Living alone, I continue to observe the festivals. I go up to the terrace every 'kanumu pongal' even now and place the rice balls on a paper

---

65   Kumkum – vermilion powder that Hindu women apply on their foreheads after marriage

66   Chakkarepongal – Main Pongal dish prepared with rice, milk, sugar / jaggery, spices and nuts

plate facing eastward and pray for my two brothers' wellbeing. After a blistering summer followed by soothing rains, it still seems like a season of festivals, right from end August through till mid-April. Whatever be my state of health I unfailingly celebrate every one of these festivals.

One of Amma's many unspoken talents was singing. She had trained in Carnatic vocal music and was an excellent singer. If she was not bound by family and responsibilities I think she would have been a famous singer. She taught me the basics and I would sit with her when the teacher came for her singing class. I was hardly any match for her but loved those sessions. As Appa's drinking bouts grew worse she would often sit in a room with her 'tambura[67]' and sing. When she was totally immersed in the music, Appa would quietly go and bolt the door of the room from outside and walk off.

Amma suffered from a fear of closed rooms and he loved to shake her out of her pleasant mood by rousing this fear in her. I remember coming back from college one afternoon and as I placed my bag down in the living room, heard a whimpering from one of the rooms. Appa in a drunken state had locked Amma in the room where she was practicing her music and having done the deed, he was lying in bed. When I saw the nervous state Amma was in, I lost my temper completely and marching up to his bed, I woke him up, splashed cold water on his face and threatened him that if he ever harmed Amma again I would kill him. The ways in which he tortured her make my hair stand on end even as I recall them now. I used to sleep beside her with an arm round her whenever Appa went on his drinking bout in order to prevent any act of violence. Even then he would come silently and catch hold of her hair

---

[67] Tambura – musical instrument to help set and maintain the pitch of vocal / instrumental Indian music

from between the bars of the bed post and pull it. Not wanting to disturb me and I think also out of shame, she tried to keep silent for as long as possible but suddenly she would whimper out of pain and I would wake up and push him out of the room. He would return silently and prick the soles of her feet with pins and again I would wake up and slap him and send him to bed.

One summer, when we were sleeping on the floor of the balcony due to the oppressive heat, I found that he was walking on her back. I was so upset I could have killed him then. I could never understand his feeling for Amma because he was undoubtedly very fond of her. This was yet another example of domestic violence that I saw at very close quarters and I vowed I would never let anyone touch a hair on my head.

He was very pleasant with her when sober but something changed when he was drunk. Sometimes he would be drunk for days together, making a mess all around him. Somewhere in my heart I felt sorry for him and would wait till he was done, get him out of the binge slowly and he would be alright for some months at a stretch. He never seemed to feel any craving during these long gaps. Then all of a sudden, he would start getting irritable, using abusive language, pick up a quarrel with Amma for no reason at all, and then he was on another binge. One blessing in all this was that he never ever misbehaved with me either by word or touch. That is what made me overlook the tension of his alcoholism. Given that some of my uncles were such sleazy people, he was refreshingly different, never took advantage of me, and that helped me retain my sanity, sense of balance and faith in the universe to a large extent.

My father, besides being lower middle class Brahmin, was also a brief less barrister for a very long time and later on even when he started getting a good clientele he did not lose his sense of being a failure in life. He seems to have aspired to have more means than he actually had and that probably led to loss of self-confidence which he tried to drown in liquor. His expertise and insight must have been good because his clients were well known companies, the railways, the airlines and a host of city businessmen.

I remember visiting one of his clients in Hyderabad and telling him that Appa was a hopeless alcoholic and a no-good lawyer and this man said that he would never telephone our home again asking for my father but that I should not speak on matters that I knew nothing about. He gave me a tolerant smile and said that Appa had saved his business and he had nothing but respect for him. It was the same case with every other client. If I took a telephone call and said that my father was lying drunk, the person at the other end would merely say 'OK, when he gets up tell him that I called.'

There may have been some reason for his getting into alcoholism but his professional expertise was respected till a few months before he died at the ripe age of 86. Except for this one habit which he managed to kick only very late in life, it appeared to me he was a wonderful person, loving spouse, caring father, good friend and respected person in society. An example of his popularity is that when he passed on his membership in Nawab Club, an elite club in Hyderabad to me, both senior club members and staff recognized the membership number and would come up and ask me if I was Ramachar sir's daughter.

If one asks me what relevance does Appa's alcoholism have in my life, I would say that it has made me totally intolerant of people who advocate tolerance of violence in men who are under the influence of liquor. I get agitated when anyone says that men usually beat up their women because they are not in their senses and that they should be treated sensitively. Having seen the pattern of violent behavior Appa resorted to, it disturbs me that men literally get away with murder.

After a long delay, we finally got over our examinations and I performed exceedingly well. My mind was set on doing my Masters in Economics in Prince University. But Appa was determined to send me to work. His drinking was so bad that he wanted to be free of the burden of running the house. This was despite the fact that Thatha used to regularly get money from his younger brother for running the house. My elder brother Kavi who had taken up a job as Sales Representative, did not want me to go against my ambition to study further, though I thought that it was best to take up a job.

Scanning the newspapers for job vacancies, I spotted an advertisement in the newspapers announcing a walk - in interview in some hotel in Hyderabad. I went there by bus. Kavi followed me on his motorbike. He walked in just as I was about to go for the interview, sat me down in the lobby and asked if I really wanted to work. I broke down and said I wanted to study further. He said so you will, come on; let's get out of this seedy joint. I went to Prince University the next day, got the admission forms, filled them in and submitted them. Kavi gave me the money for the fees.

Two thoughts always remain in my mind. One is that with so little money so much was possible. The other is that here was my brother who never resented me though Appa always berated him for poor academic performance; he was actually proud of me though he was just two and half years older than me; he found it necessary to take up a job immediately after graduation in order to help Amma with the household expenses, yet he held no rancor and he was so determined that I should pursue my studies. But for his support at that juncture I would have been a receptionist in some hotel or a salesgirl in a textile showroom. With my post graduate studies started another of my exciting phases in life.

Entering Prince University was for me like entering heaven. The gates of learning, I felt then, opened up there. It was also the emergence of young adults, expansion of minds, birth of new thoughts, articulation of these thoughts, common thinking, discussions, putting thoughts and discussions into a political framework. The grand structure and magnificence of the campus provided the impetus for us to develop our thoughts and pursue them into discussions, sometimes with the august faculty and sometimes among ourselves. I literally could not keep my feet on the ground. This was serious academic pursuit. I had applied for Economics and had a counseling session with the head of the department Professor Gambhir. The fact that my performance at the graduate level was exceedingly good assured him that I would do the department proud.

In all, we were 26 students of whom 4 were girls. We girls formed one group. Rita was a fidgety, giggling person who was not quite sure why she chose to do a Master's degree in the first place; she eventually changed her subject and went on to study Public Administration. She however kept in touch with us and once invited me for a tea party at her place. It was a variety of vegetable and chutney sandwiches with tea and biscuits; the sandwiches were cut into so many intricate and interesting shapes, all the size of small pastries, it was fascinating. I have tried but never succeeded in my efforts to make similar sandwiches.

It was in my M.A. that my shorthand training came in use. I used to take down notes in shorthand and then transcribe the same into long hand, making two carbon copies so Sheela and Parimala could have one set each. They in turn would do the library reference work and make a set of notes for me. This shared work was an excellent arrangement and helped us. The boys did not know what we were up to but we always performed well, be it written assignments or tests. Sheela unfortunately stopped attending classes after a few months. I visited her home and was surprised to see such a small place and so many people living in it. I was told by her mother that Sheela's marriage had been fixed and so what was the use of continuing her studies. I tried convincing her and then it was agreed that if after marriage, her husband did not object, she could continue her studies. He did not and she resumed classes. I helped her to make up for the lost time. But very soon she got pregnant and was too sick most of the time to come to class.

Parimala and I were the only two girls left and we soon became inseparable friends. In the beginning, she came rather overdressed, and I casually remarked that it was alright to go for outings dressed that way but did not seem appropriate for an Economics Masters class. She understood my point and altered her dress code. What I appreciated about the university campus in those days was that while the teaching faculty would show their disapproval at the most by not making eye contact with a girl dressed boldly, even the students did not ridicule or tease her. It must have been difficult for both the teachers and the students in the department to be so well behaved, considering that we were the only two females in an all-male crowd. On the part of the staff I can confidently say that there was never any attempt to harass us; and the students treated us as one of them. Parimala's other graduate school friends had all opted for English as their subject and in those days the English Masters students always looked down upon the rest of us! We were both housed in the Arts building. I was looked down upon by her set of friends! Parimala initially tried to get me into her crowd but sensing my discomfiture, she tried splitting her time between them and me for a short period. Finally, somehow it so happened that we spent a lot more time together and became inseparable friends, till her untimely death.

Parimala was a pretty girl with a lovely dimple and ever smiling face, and one could literally hear the swoons of the boys when she entered the campus corridors. She was always quite breathless about the excitement and flutter she caused. When I teased her about it she would ask 'do you really mean it? Am I really beautiful?' and I would say 'Not beautiful in that sense but pretty, yes.' She always struck me as wanting constant reassurance about her looks. I could not quite understand why. For me it was only my academics that mattered. I could not understand why she was so anxious about her appearance because she was a very good student and came from a highly educated and elite family. I have always thought that it is our academic or work performance that should get appreciated and did not really bother about my looks. It may be that I was the odd one out or I was fortunate enough to not need such reassurance! I remember visiting their home for the first time and was surprised to see uniformed butlers serving us lunch. She loved coming home and my parents grew very fond of her.

The Economics department had the cream of faculty and students in that academic year. The teacher – student ratio was good and we were able to actually have conversations with our professors on a one on one basis on subject related issues. There were four boys in competition with us. One boy was the nephew of one of our Professors and he was always sure of topping the class. There were active student unions, particularly in the Arts and Engineering colleges. The leaders were all some Reddy or other. Parimala and I stayed out of it all, but because of Parimala's courteous attitude of responding to any greeting with a smile, we got into something of a mess with the one of the boys. This guy had a 'crush' on her and was sending her messages to visit him when he was lying in hospital with a fractured leg. She panicked and I did too. We somehow wriggled ourselves out of the situation but I was really scared and sternly warned her not to be friendly with any boy on the campus thereafter.

Our first year examinations were fast approaching and I was confident of topping the class. However, it turned out that my classmate Narsimha topped by just a few marks. I was somehow not happy and was urged by Asha and Rajamama to ask for a revaluation, if I was confident. The risk was that I would probably invite the prejudice of the faculty. I asked for a revaluation and it turned out that I scored the highest marks. I did not bother to probe further since I had got the justice I wanted. Just a few months after the commencement of the second year, there was an announcement of the entrance examination for the Probationary Officers post in National Bank of India.

Goaded by Appa's jeering that I could never compete in such areas like the civil services and bank officers' competitive examinations, I submitted my application for the National Bank of India's competitive examination and completed the written examination. I had not prepared for it at all, but I was among the 12 who qualified for the interview. At the interview, the Chairman asked me why I did not complete my Masters and appear for the examination in the coming year and I answered that if that was what I wanted to do, I would not have applied at all. He smiled and I left the room. The next thing I knew, I had been selected and was asked to go for my medicals. Here the first glitch appeared. My urine test revealed traces of albumin and my appointment was stayed till the medical clearance came through. After almost a month and two more medical tests, the clearance came through and I reported for duty at the National Bank of India Main Branch on Bankers Street in Hyderabad. Everyone at home was happy and Thatha was so thrilled that he took me shopping one evening and bought me a whole lot of saris! He wanted that his 'brilliant' granddaughter wear a new sari every day of the coming year! The money for all this of course came from his younger brother who was a flourishing businessman in Delhi.

I had the regret of leaving my Masters midway. My attendance was adequate enough for me to write the examination even while working but I knew it would not be the same as attending classes. My Professor Gambhir was unhappy that I was taking up a job in the first place, since he saw me as the next Gambhir and had planned my PhD topic, thesis and all!

It was November 1970 and I remember the first day in my first ever job. I stood waiting to report outside the Personnel Manager's room in the Regional Office waiting to be called in and formally inducted. He took his own time and I kept waiting. He finally came out to leave for somewhere and finding me waiting, went back to his room, spoke on the phone and asked me to report to the manager in the Main Branch adjoining the Regional Office. Again, it was an eternity before the gentleman raised his head from the massive ledger in front of him and absently asked me 'What?' 'Reporting for duty, sir,' I replied and handed my letter of appointment. He muttered something about what a nuisance POs[68] were.

In the 1970s when I joined, the animosity the promotee officers had towards the direct recruits or POs was so obvious and incomprehensible for us at first glance. Never one to keep silent, I asked the branch manager why we were discriminated against and he looked aghast and said discriminated – who is discriminated – look at me I have been working so hard since

---

[68]   PO – Probationary Officer

I was 20, joined as a clerk and now at 40+ I am manager. You people write an examination, pass it and then we have to help you do a crash course in fundamentals of banking which people like me learnt by slogging for so many years for such low salaries. At the end of it all you will sit on my head and order me about before I retire. I quite understood the resentment.

This resentment was so bad it could have made or broken our careers. A negative report from the manager at the end of the induction and our fate would be sealed. The fact that I was female made it worse. There were hardly any women in the bank itself in the early 1970s and we were only four officers in the Regional Office of whom three were recent recruits. Rima, Seeta and I – Sasmita joined a month or so later. This first job, despite all the problems was intoxicating. I always felt my feet were three feet above the ground. I don't know if I walked like that too because I remember Ammama telling me once that I walked on my toes rather than on my feet! Maybe I felt on top of the world most of the time in those days. I was particularly thrilled when I heard that four of my male class mates from the university had also attempted the examination in the same year but not succeeded - I truly felt like a Nobel Prize laureate!

Everything at work was new and exciting. However much anyone tried to dampen my spirits, I was on a high. I would always arrive at the office a bit early since it was drilled into our heads from childhood that punctuality meant being a bit early at the spot and making oneself seen at the appointed time. In the bank everyone walked in slowly after 10.30 a.m. and they took their own time getting settled; then we got our morning coffee/tea. The beverage had to be given undivided attention for some time and then after a couple of sips the guys would greet each other, exchange pleasantries. I would be sitting or standing around with a stupid grin on my face; it was amazing how they invisibilised me. Right there was I, all of 5 feet, four and half inches tall with a long thick plait falling down my back and how can I not be there? If I was in the way, they would go round me, just stand close so I moved and made way, but they did not utter a word to me. Sheetal was also in the same branch but in some other section, which meant that I could not go across and sit with her.

When I went to the toilet I would again be met with silence and sense the gazes moving away. Finally, I smiled tentatively at one young woman Komala outside the bathroom and quickly befriended her. Komala was Tamil Brahmin, which at that point of time gave me a lot of comfort and reassurance. Hierarchy and conservatism played such an important role in the work culture of my very first job. Komala and I boarded the same bus at the terminus quite often and I would sit beside her, chatting away, enter the office together with her and I also started sitting with her during lunch time.

Rima one day told me that our senior colleague Revathi wanted to meet me during lunch and so I went across to the officers' lounge; it was a huge and spacious room and I took some time spotting Revathi. She looked me up head to toe and took her own time inviting me to sit across her. She made some small conversation with difficulty and then said 'Coming to the point, Usha, officers don't sit and lunch with, or mingle freely with 'award staff.' The point did not register in my brain and then she half smiled and said that my sitting with Komala and the clerks during lunch was inappropriate. I asked where I should sit for lunch. She said that I could use the officers' lounge and it was not necessary for me to carry lunch since the meal there was subsidized. I looked around and felt truly terrified and at sea. I made it a point to join Rima every day from then on, but carried my lunch box. I could never befriend Revathi.

The laughter and chatter of the clerical staff lunch room was so energizing and I think, also a necessary break from the monotony of the first half of a working day, but that kind of fun was never there in the officers' lounge. Even the men did not laugh boisterously, unless it was a senior officer who was cracking a joke and all the juniors laughed because they were expected to. In the midst of getting settled in my new surroundings, I was told that I would have to go for the Orientation Course, which was a five week residential training. I was barely one week old into my job. It was explained that the candidate originally selected was pregnant and could not travel, so I was selected in order to complete the required size of the training batch. Luckily for me, the training was in Hyderabad. My hopes of being able to commute to and from home were crashed because it was strictly residential. And so the training at Black Rock, View Point Road started.

We were 4 girls and 20 boys, I think. They were from all over the country and all of them were from the previous batch of recruits. Except for one person we were all in the same age group. We girls were accommodated two to a room and I got a room on the first floor. Rima was my roommate. Sheetal and Sudha shared a room on the ground floor. The rooms were spacious and airy. The classroom, dining hall and sitting room were on the ground floor. We had two instructors. The boys were all decent and also lost no time in bonding together among themselves. A few of them were reserved but the boisterous lot drew everyone into a fit of laughter with their antics.

Every Saturday I would go home at lunch, with all my accumulated laundry and come back on Sunday evening with a fresh set of clothes for the next week! It became a standing joke at the training centre that I was a delicate darling and not used to work – which was of course, true. In class, one of the instructors took an instant dislike to me and would lose no opportunity to ask me some question which I did not know the answer to. I had just about completed one week in my job and did not know the basics of banking. He would remark that girls like me just came to while away our time and we were taking up jobs in which process other deserving candidates were denied an opportunity. This man was married to the daughter of Appa's friend and it seems he used to go and report that I was not serious about my work. Appa did not tell me all this until a quite few years later. I found it peculiar that the man was so resentful of me.

As it is, just having beauty and brains and freely mixing with boys labeled a girl as being empty headed, flirtatious and 'available'. I did not bother about the disapproving looks from the faculty outside of class but their constant effort to humiliate me in class was very painful; there was nothing I could do about it since my knowledge of practical banking was minimal. We were a carefree bunch and had a lot of fun outside of class, getting to know each other. Some of the boys were reserved and kept a distance with us girls but there was a group with really fun guys and one of them, Arijit, I ended up marrying a year later. The other colleagues are leading their own lives and I hardly hear about them.

From what I gleaned at that training, girls and boys do come for such trainings with an intention of finding a spouse, since it is one opportunity when they can get to know each other; the other reason for this 'hidden agenda' is that usually, boy and girls who get into the IAS[69] or National Bank as officers, find it easy to be married to someone from the same background. The reasons are that they are equally qualified,

---

[69] IAS – Indian Administrative Services

have a common interest in terms of career, and of course it is financial security for both partners.

Unfortunately, none of these reasons prompted me to get involved with Arijit. It was his gentleness, lovely voice, and interest in English literature. Rima was into serious husband hunting and therefore went all out to check on a potential partner for herself! Meanwhile, my health started playing up because it was winter and I had a sudden bout of rheumatic pain. One morning I woke up with high fever and pain in every single joint. It was only in that excruciating pain, I realized how many joints the human body has. I could not speak, move my head or neck. Rima got worried and I just signaled her to arrange an autorickshaw to take me to Dr. Chinnana. She accompanied me and was very irritated when she saw where I had brought her, feeling that I should get into a hospital. Dr. Chinnana's clinic was an overstuffed, untidy room with creaky windows in a section of his sprawling house. It gave an impression of being on the verge of collapse.

As he opened the door and glanced at me the doctor understood what was wrong. Tears of pain were streaming down my cheeks. He felt my pulse and then mixed some tinctures and powdered sugar and gave me one dose right away. He said that every half hour I should take one dose and assured that in two hours I would be totally alright. He asked that I rest for the morning. We went back and Rima, seeing the improvement in me with one dose said, 'I don't believe this,' but she had to, when she saw the improvement in two hours. She told the faculty that I was sick and would attend the afternoon session if I was well enough. She reported back to me that it was not well received, but I was feeling too ill and tired, to even be bothered.

Dr. Chinnana telephoned Appa and informed that I was ill. Appa's concern was only that I may lose my job. Amma revealed to me later that it was not an affectionate concern about my health but that loss of the job would mean loss of the income for him. I had not thought of my income as yet and said she was just imagining things. Later however, I realized that Appa always had this worry about running out of money. Amma was very worried about my coping alone at the training center and insisted that I ask for permission to come home. I was too scared to ask if it was possible and also, I had started feeling better so I stayed on. My colleagues at the training centre did not understand what was wrong with me and I made no attempt to explain it either. Maybe I should have and Arijit would not have pursued his romantic interest in me.

Explaining my illnesses continues to be a problem even now and I try to push it behind, get on with whatever I am doing. I could see this streak in Akhil Patil, whose lower limbs had been affected by polio. He was initially very bristly when any of us showed concern, but he slowly found his comfort level and proved to be great company with a warm heart and cheerful laughter. We were all aware of the fact that he was annoyed with himself for his condition and were very sensitive to it; we never attempted to show sympathy, only helping him when he asked for it. This is something I learnt at Black Rock – to be empathetic rather than sympathetic.

The four weeks were soon coming to an end and while I was looking forward to going back home and to family, I did feel a bit sad that we were all going our different directions and we may or may not keep in touch. On the closing day the Chairman presided over the closing function and in his farewell address to us, said that we were the cream of the cream of society and should always endeavor to give our best to the bank. It pleased us all greatly that we were referred to as the cream of the cream and I truly felt special. Arijit and I sang a duet from the Hindi film 'Pyasa' as part of the cultural programme. Before leaving Black Rock, we all took a group photograph and each of us wrote something on the reverse of each other's copy. I got the first open 'confession' of interest from Arijit in the form of the verse he wrote on my copy of the photograph. 'I came to the land of rocks, and found a dainty flower, whose image will drive away sorrows in the times ahead.' I don't remember what I wrote. We all promised to keep in touch.

I went home where everybody was busy with his or her own thing and nobody asked what happened at the training or what I felt. I got prepared to start attending office once again. While the induction course was too early for me and I did not perform well in the training, I think it helped me tackle my work better; it helped set my comfort level at work. It was a true job induction and prepared me for the task on hand. My self-confidence with respect to the work must have been obvious because the attitude and approach of the counter staff towards me changed. I knew what I was expected to do instead of wasting time trying to figure it out with the unhelpful staff around me. I moved more easily and at the counter, I did not maintain the 'stiff upper lip' demeanor. I had to master the basics of banking and it would not have been possible if I maintained my distance as an officer. This attitude helped me tremendously since the counter staff were very co-operative once I showed them that I looked towards them for support and guidance; I was able to move through each counter smoothly and complete my tasks confidently and on time. Quite often, seeing that I was able to manage the counter work, the clerks used to ask me to manage their counters and disappear for their coffee and cigarette breaks frequently. They would come late in the morning knowing I would have started setting things in place.

Thinking back on that phase many years later, I realized that there were always attempts from the staff to romance me, starting from the messenger boys to the officers. Since I was relaxed and friendly some of them would usually start with complaints about problems on the home front. They would complain about their families and the lack of an understanding wife and I would pass it off with a light banter or behave as if I had not heard. One messenger boy actually proposed marriage to me and I simply said that it was too early for me to think of marriage and thank you very much. Another counter clerk suddenly said to me that he dreamt of me the whole night! I was determined not to let anything get me down and brushed off all these advances in a good humored way.

All this apart, there was one officer who had been eyeing me, as I made the rounds from one counter to the other, waiting for me to go to his table. I hated the idea of going to his section but it was unavoidable, since I had to get his clearance also. He would make me sit in front of him day after day and not show me the different steps involved in something as simple as making a fixed deposit. The blank receipts were usually safely locked away. It was with the help of a sympathetic counter clerk that I learnt the different steps involved in making a fixed deposit. The officer would always make me wait till 7 or 8 p.m. on the pretext of having a lot of work. Being a junior officer in his section I could not walk out before he did. It frightened me to be in that empty hall with him and invariably he would ask me if he could drop me home in his car. I would just say that my father was waiting for me outside and then quietly slip across to the bus stop. Once I had just reached the bus stop and found the officer bending over across the front seat of his car and asking if wanted a 'lift.' I smilingly refused, saying my father would still turn up. There were hardly any people at the bus stop at 8 p.m. in those days. It was scary that he followed me and even more scary that if I acted rudely I could lose my job.

One day I mustered up enough courage to tell him that I knew how to make a fixed deposit. He smiled derisively and asked me to go ahead and show him. I sat at the counter, and from the first step of talking with the customer on the other side of the counter regarding details of the kind of fixed deposit he wished to make, I proceeded step by step and completed the entire process upto writing the receipt. He meanwhile visited the manager. When he returned I showed him the receipt, and since there was no mistake, he had to give me clearance so I could move on to the next section.

The last part of the training was that of balancing the daily cash book. This was a very tricky affair. Firstly, it is never easy to balance it at the end of the day. The other problem we as women probationers faced were antics by the counter staff or messenger boys hiding payment slips. One of my colleagues struggled for a week and left without balancing the cash book. I came to know that one of the messenger boys had hidden a payment slip which was why she couldn't complete her task. He carried a grudge against her just because she had spoken with him curtly..

The sexism prevalent then was mindboggling. Balancing the cash book was easy for me fortunately and I was glad not to have antagonized any of the staff. By this time Seeta Iyer had joined. She was initially a bit uptight with the award staff and had a tough time till she heeded my words and started being more friendly with them. One positive aspect was that we were now four officers, including Revathi and so we were able to sit at a table in the officers' lounge during lunch time.

The only reason I liked the officers' lounge was that it had very nice clean toilets and I needed this particularly when I had my periods. With the heavy bleeding I needed to change at least four times during the working day and it was such a blessing to have a clean bathroom with plenty of water and a trashcan where I could dump my soiled pads.

Arijit and I had started corresponding and his letters were very interesting; very neat handwriting, excellent English and so descriptive of Darjeeling where he was posted. I often feel I have lived in Darjeeling because of his letters. He is an excellent writer. I would write about Hyderabad and we always found something beautiful to exchange in our letters rather than mundane office matters or simply filling the letter with 'I love you...' It was intellect meeting intellect. I was posted to Gopalapuram in May 1971, having completed six months in my first posting. Arijit sent me a telegram that he would come from Kharagpur where he had got his third posting, to meet me, on the 18th of June. I did not know that my father had read the telegram and gone into a fit of nervousness. In a hurry my parents decided to persuade my sister Asha to accompany me and to arrange for me to be temporarily accommodated in her friend Raju's home. We reached on the 17th of June and I reported for duty.

My colleague Rima also got her second posting in the same branch of the city a month prior to me and she had settled into a nice house overlooking the sea. I told Rima that Arijit was arriving on 18th and I would go to the railway station to meet him and if she could cover for me at the office for the forenoon I would report for work by the afternoon. It turned out that Arijit's train was inordinately late so I returned to office and then came back to the railway station around

4 p.m. when the train finally reached. Even at that point of time, I was not sure what I felt when I met him. We were both feeling quite odd and at a loss as to the next step. He needed to have a bath and so checked into Park View Hotel. I went into the room with him and sat waiting on the bed while he freshened up. I asked if he was hungry and he said something utterly silly and clichéd like 'hungry for you…' Then he sat down beside me and started kissing me and I sat, not knowing what to do. I was quite naïve when it came to getting physical. It was getting dark and I said that I would have to go. And he said something like, 'let's get married…' and I asked when and he said 'tomorrow…' I laughed and he said, 'seriously.' I was restless and worried that it was around 9 p.m. and I neither had the telephone number of our host's home nor the exact address.

We got out of the hotel and found a cycle rickshaw. Somehow, I managed to locate the house and got out promising to meet him at 9 a.m. the next day. I walked into the house and my sister Asha came running to the door, scared as to what may have happened to me and angry that I was so late. I just went in and said, 'I'm getting married to Arijit tomorrow.' Her mouth fell open. She said I must be joking and I said no I was dead serious. She went in and I think told her friend Raju about the predicament she was in. She asked if she could phone Amma in Hyderabad to convey the news. Amma seems to have said that I was a stubborn mule and to just please get me married in as decent a manner as possible. Asha sat and wept after the call. It seems that Appa had woken up and on hearing of my decision, threatened to jump into our well at home. I secretly thought it would be a good riddance… our host Raju came in and asked if I was sure and I said yes and he said then we would be married properly, in the Lakshmi Narsimhaswamy temple in Simhachalam and he and his wife Uma would give me away, in the absence of my parents. He then asked me where Arijit was staying and I told him the name of the hotel. He grimaced and then in no time tracked the hotel and asked to speak with Arijit; he asked Arijit his shirt size and told him to be ready and waiting at the hotel by 10 a.m. from where we would pick him up. Raju brusquely asked, 'I hope you know that Usha is going to be married to you.' I felt guilty at having put my sister, her friend and his wife in a spot.

That night I don't think any of us really slept. Raju's wife was a hypertensive and very conservative person, and this turn of events, as a result of her having agreed to have us as house guests, must have left her completely at a loss. Raju probably conjectured that I had already got into a relationship with Arijit and this was the best solution in case I got pregnant. Though they had not met he did not seem to trust Arijit at all.

When I thought back about our marriage a few months later, I also wondered if, left to himself Arijit would have married me at all. He probably saw that I was quite conservative about how physical I would get in a relationship and concluded that marriage was the only way to get physically intimate with me. I was so confused and immature. Just because I had stayed out with Arijit till 9 in the night I felt that I should get married and thereby solemnize what happened (or did not happen). I felt even then that Arijit and I had behaved immaturely and got ourselves into a relationship in haste.

The next morning Raju went to the hotel and picked up Arijit (before he could run away) and Uma took me shopping to buy me a new sari and the mangalsutra.[70] We all went in a car to the temple in Simhachalam. I remember that Kiran, my nephew was with us and he was so attached to me he would not let go of my hand. The wedding took place and we bundled into the car. Raju promised me that he would collect the marriage certificate from the temple and asked where we wanted to get dropped. I said I did not know. He took us to Hotel Apsara and asked for a room to be given to us and I wished Asha and Kiran goodbye. The child was suffering from a severe stomach upset and I was very upset at leaving the child like that. He was crying aloud as they drove away. Arijit was annoyed on the whole. I just wanted to go back to console my favourite nephew.

We went into the hotel and everyone from the bellboy to the guests in the lobby were giving us leering looks. Once we reached the room, Arijit led me to the bed and I don't remember anything much except a lot of pain. Later, he stood at the window and smoked. I was tired and hungry and dazed by the turn of events since the previous evening. Later on we went out to the beach and ate some peanuts. We decided that we should intimate all our relatives that we were married. Each of us made a list and then went to the telegraph office and sent the telegrams. Back at the hotel, we went into the restaurant for dinner and whom should I bump into but one of Appa's cousins! I blandly introduced Arijit as my husband and walked ahead. I was so sensitive and resentful about the circumstances and felt that everyone would be able to see that I had sex with Arijit and for some reason felt ashamed and guilty about it at that point of time.

---

[70] Mangalsutra – the sacred thread / chain tied by the bridegroom round the bride's neck at time of marriage; symbol of marriage for Hindu women

The next morning I went over to meet Rima and explain to her what had happened. On her advice I went over to the office with Arijit and explained to the manager that we had got married and since Arijit was staying only two more days in the city I requested for two days' leave. I knew that I could not continue to stay on in a hotel and there was no other place for me to go to. I asked Rima if I could share her accommodation and split the rent with her. She was not happy because she disapproved of the way I had got married and also worried that if Arijit landed up every now and then he would naturally expect to stay with us and though I was married to him there would be questions raised by the house owners and neighbors about her as a single woman staying with us. I assured her that Arijit would not come and stay with us and make it awkward for her. Arijit left and I moved in with Rima.

The house Rima had taken on rent was a very nice one and from the rear verandah we had a lovely view of the beach and the blue expanse of sea. I was not a great cook but Rima was worse than me. She would hold a brinjal up and look at it from all sides, and then she would place it on the chopping board and wielding the knife she would look at me and ask how she should chop it! In my letters home I narrated our housekeeping efforts. Amma was able to discern our plight and she offered to come and take care of us. It was a wonderful arrangement.

Rima immediately took to Amma and there was one more probationer Sasmita, who joined us the following month. So the three of us would hand over housekeeping money to Amma every month and the three of us split Amma's expenses between us. For the other two this seemed better than paying her something every month. At the office I was seen as a brazen creature who just went off and married someone of my own will and that too, a non-Brahmin.

It was not common for Brahmins to marry outside the caste and in fact even marrying across the sub sects within the Brahmin community was frowned upon. The general assumption was that I must have got into some 'trouble,' and hence the hasty wedding. The branch manager and senior officers were openly looking at my stomach to see if I was showing signs of pregnancy! Just the fact of my getting married sealed my fate. I would go early and the 'dak' as the mail was referred to in those days in banking parlance, would be hidden from me; the manager would find fault with me for not doing the assigned work. I was sent to the loans and advances department and the officer in charge behaved as if I did not exist at all. It was very embarrassing and tormenting. Nevertheless, I persisted in continuing my efforts to complete my probation.

My total transformation post marriage puzzles me even as I write now. How did it happen that Arijit, the husband, continued to remain 'intellect' and I changed overnight into 'woman/wife'? Suddenly our roles were defined differently. How did it happen and who defined these roles puzzled me since I was always someone who stood out of the general crowd.

I remembered when I was doing my post-graduation, a friend of my sister had come to the university to pick me up one afternoon - he drove straight up to me, leant across, opened the door and asked me to get in saying he was sent by my sister. He then introduced himself. When we reached her place she asked him if he had any difficulty finding me and he said 'no, you said to look around and the girl who stands out in the whole crowd is your sister, and so I found her…' It thrilled me no end to hear that my sister had said this about me!

Immediately after marriage I experienced a fall from that special status, which undoubtedly I did enjoy. There was a specialness I had as a person always and suddenly this seemed to disappear. Is this the price one pays for love and marriage, I asked myself and if it is why did I have to pay the price? My husband continued to be intellect but related to me as 'man' to 'woman.' I was 'woman, wife, daughter-in-law, sister-in-law.' The sexual relationship not only altered equations between the two of us but marriage made me a lesser being in the society I moved. There was a code of conduct that crept into my conscious and subconscious levels. I was suddenly made conscious of my stride while walking, the width to which my lips stretched when I smiled, and the sound of my laughter.

I can't say I became conscious, it is just that something made me conscious all of a sudden. There was a feeling that I belonged to somebody. Why, I asked myself, when I never felt so earlier? I could have belonged to my parents, grandparents, but it was not so. I was born, grew, gained education, but I was never someone's possession. This particular sense was driven into me with a suddenness and force exactly one month into my marriage. I started worrying about displeasing the man whom I married for love. His unarticulated mistrust, long silences, moping stride had me totally stumped. I became conscious of the sound of my own laughter, and the sparkle in my eyes had started dying. Why did I not simply call it quits immediately? I don't know.

I don't know if it would have been different had I married someone from my own community, region and social background. What I could see was that as far as my own family was concerned, I continued to be an integral part of it all through. But with Arijit I could see we were certainly growing apart, and I was becoming cautious, scared and uncertain about everything. Two months after marriage Arijit came to Kalingapatnam and we both went on my first visit to Bhubaneswar in order to meet his family.

Amma came to the railway station to see me off and she cried while standing on the railway platform. It did not occur to me then that she was crying as a mother would cry when she gives her daughter away in marriage. For me it was just a week of meeting his family and then returning to my home and job, but she saw it as my departure from my maternal home. It was only once I returned that I asked her the reason for crying and Rima asked how I could be so dumb as to not understand a mother's grief at marrying off a daughter. This is a sentiment that still does not make any sense because I firmly believe that a child always has a place in her/his home however old one grows. In retrospect, maybe I knew I would never really go away from my hometown and family!

As our train rolled into Bhubaneswar at the unearthly hour of around 4 a.m., I was in for a total shock. We got down and stood in the dim light of the railway platform; a woman walked up to me and then draped my sari pallav over my head. She then held my hands up for inspection and muttering something she hurriedly slipped some of her glass bangles on to my wrists. Arijit simply walked ahead with two other men (who were later introduced to me as his elder brothers), and I was following with their wives, one on either side of me. They asked me something in a language I could not follow. One of the women was as tall as me and the other was short. Outside the railway station I was pushed into the back seat of a car and the other two women got in on either side of me.

Arijit had told me that when his mother came to greet me I should bend and touch her feet. I was brought up to not touch anyone's feet, but I had seen Amma go down on her haunches and bend her body forward touching her forehead to the floor in front of either the deities we worshipped, or the elders as and when necessary. She would do this twice in quick succession. So when I was taken to his mother I did what I had seen Amma doing. It was tricky doing it with the sari covering my head and there were so many people I had to keep doing it to. It was some years later when my respect for the relationship itself had completely got lost that I adopted the style prevalent in his community and region – that of bending from the waist down and touching the feet with the tips of my fingers. I had a good laugh at myself many years later when I recalled how I would hurriedly go down on my haunches and duck my head not twice but four times at the feet of every elder in the family!

The son preference and repeatedly endorsed importance of men over women came across to me in every little aspect of family life in my marital home. If I wanted a bath I had to wait till the men finished their baths. The women would eat only after the men had eaten. In fact there was an expectation that I would eat off Arijit's plate, but my shocked look must have dispelled the thought off my mother - in -law's mind! I was not to show my face to the men in the family. The women's voices would not be heard in the presence of the men.

On my first visit, we had actually gone to stay in the home of Arijit's eldest brother Shoorveer, who was an officer in the civil services; he was married to a very lovely woman called Latika, who is the cousin of a local politician of repute. Shoorveer pacing up and down the living room told me that all the sons in the Pathi family, of their generation, had to have the second name of Veer, so Arijit was Arijit Veer and so on. He humorously gave me a briefing on the family background. The house was full of people on that first visit because Arijit's siblings and their families had dropped in to 'see' his bride. I was taken to the main bedroom of the house and pushed by the shoulder to sit on the edge of the bed. I was irked as to why I had to be held or pushed all the time, since I felt people could have communicated to me verbally as to what I should do.

After what seemed an eternity, I was allowed to go into the bathroom and complete my morning ablutions. Once I came out, I was asked to dress in a silk sari – I had not envisioned there would be so many people or that any religious or social formalities were lined up and not brought any. Lekha gave me one of her saris which matched a blouse I had carried. They pushed a whole lot of red bangles onto both my wrists and then smeared my heels with a red paint called 'alta.[71]' The sari pallav was once again pulled over my head. Arijit did not come into the room at all. His brother Shoor came in and engaged in a conversation with me. It felt good to be talking with someone in English. The faltering Hindi and the totally alien Oriya of the women were wearing me down. They kept asking about my jewelry and I said they were all in my bank locker.

Arijit's other elder brother Ranveer was a shy type but he also spoke caringly. Both Shoor and Ranveer ribbed each other and Arijit jovially, and I joined in the laughter. Suddenly Arijit came in with a bristling temper, the cause of which I did not know. An elderly gentleman came and stood at the door and I went and offered my obeisance when someone told me that he was Arijit's father. Another equally old man came and I did the same thing. This falling to my knees I must have done over 50 times that day. I was then led to a room where there was a sacred fire lit and a Hindu priest sitting on one side. Arijit and I sat down to perform some rituals. At the end of it we walked round the sacred fire and I could not even register what the priest was saying. Once that was over, I was given a new name.

---

[71]   Alta – a red paste smeared on the edge of the feet by married women and girls and considered auspicious in Hindu rituals

Among Hindus there is a custom of changing the name of the bride once she enters her marital home.

The whole week was one of noise and anger, loud and silent (the latter was unbearable because it beamed out at me from Arijit every night). For most of the day I would be sitting on the edge of the bed, with a stream of female visitors coming and lifting the pallav to have a look at my face. Once or twice, Shoor would come in and talk with me about my family. He was a very talkative person with severe mood swings. He and Ranveer were truly a great support for me. Arijit's father also spoke chaste English but he was not allowed into the room. He used to sit on a corner stone in the outer courtyard and keep rubbing something onto his gums and then spit out red saliva. Arijit also used to spit out red saliva since he was addicted to tobacco and betel leaf and had his mouth full of it at all times except when he was eating or drinking something.

These habits were new to me. Back home, Appa used to smoke a pipe or a cigar after dinner, on the terrace and nobody smoked in the house. Betel leaf was only chewed on a festival after a heavy meal. Tobacco chewing and rubbing tobacco onto the gums must have been there even where I lived and grew up, but I tended to go around with blinkers most of the time seeing only what I wanted to see. On my first ever visit to my marital home in Bhubaneswar, I did not have the option of shutting off such scenes by closing my eyes or turning my head, since the persons chewing the stuff would stand in front of me with their mouths full of spittle, trying to make conversation and I was always tense because of the red spittle spouting out of their mouths. Later on, as I started to live in Bhubaneswar, I realized that 70% of the people I interacted with always had their mouths full of tobacco and betel leaf. The women were very demure in the presence of men but when on their own, the same chewing and loud conversation with spittle-filled mouths prevailed.

Coming back to my first visit, a few hours later in the morning, someone brought red glass bangles to fit my thin wrists, and filled the parting of my hair above my forehead with 'sindoor[72]' and I was told in very bad Hindi that I should observe purdah in front of the elders in the family and all men other than my husband and the younger male relatives. The other rules were that I should not eat before the men ate, nor should I sit when any elder entered the room be it male or female and I should keep my head bowed at all times. While all these conditions were being conveyed to me, on the one hand, on the other, Arijit had already started having some peculiar suspicion that I had not married him out of love for him but to be with another fellow trainee who lived in the same town! I did not even know who this person was or that he was in that town. It is truly peculiar that he believed I was in love with every other man except himself. There was nothing I could do about this kind of paranoia, but it took me so many years to realize that this was a sickness stemming out of his own insecurity and his way of dealing with it was by harassing me. It was so many years before I realized that I was not responsible for his suffocating suspicion. I kept agonizing over his moods and lost a precious lot of myself. His habit of dining very late and sleeping almost at dawn bothered me for many years. It felt very weird to have him pacing up and down or standing at the window smoking through the night. I would wake at 5 in the morning when he would just have fallen asleep! I was

---

[72] Sindoor – red powder smeared on the hair parting at the forehead

brought up on the 'early to bed and early to rise makes a man healthy, wealthy and wise' motto!

By the time I returned to Kalingapatnam from that first visit I knew that marrying Arijit was not a right decision. I did not know whom to talk with about it and what to do. As a result I just kept withdrawing into myself. When Amma saw the glass bangles on my wrists she frowned and asked what was that stuff I had on like a 'koothadi?[73]' I explained that I was expected to wear red bangles and she tightened her lips wordlessly. Since I was not in the company of Arijit's family I removed the glass bangles. Amma was obviously mulling over the tradition of wearing red bangles. She went on a short visit to Hyderabad a few weeks later and on her return she gave me a beautiful pair of thick gold bangles studded with imitation rubies. On my next visit to Bhubaneswar two months later, Arijit's mother ordered that some more glass bangles be given to me to wear. I showed my ruby bangles but she shook her head and I was told it should be glass or lac only. Red glass bangles were a sign of a good marriage for women according to their custom. The difference in culture between north, east and south India is so glaring. Despite the fact that I did meet and move around with friends from different regions as I grew up, my foundation was indelibly Tamil and remains so till today.

The other very Tamil practice is that of women and girls adorning their head with seasonal flowers like a single rose or a string of jasmines or chrysanthemums every day. As far back into my childhood as I can remember, all girls used to have their hair plaited in the evening and get a string of jasmines pinned in the middle of the plait. Even the older women who

---

[73]   Koothadi – dancing girl

did not have much hair but were 'sumangali'[74] would tuck in a small string of the flowers. When we moved into our home in Bhubaneswar around 1975, I remember picking the jasmines from the creeper in our garden, stringing them and wearing it in my hair - Arijit was so shocked on seeing me and abruptly asked me to remove the flowers immediately saying that only 'prostitutes' wore flowers in their hair in his part of the country. So I was a 'koothadi' if I wore glass bangles in my mother's home and a 'koothadi' if I wore jasmines in my hair in my husband's home.

Only widows covered their heads with the sari pallav in my maternal hometown and only prostitutes walked around with the sari pallav falling down the shoulder in my marital hometown. Kohl was a must for all girls and women except widows in my maternal hometown and only prostitutes lined their eyes with kohl in my marital hometown. The way I was brought up, we mingled with boys and men freely, in the sense we talked, laughed and ate together.

The customs practiced in my marital home surfaced on my very first visit to my marital home. I could not allow my elder male relatives to look at my face. The men ate first and then Arijit's youngest sister put out one plate, served the food and said let's eat. This shocked my senses because I was not used to sharing a plate – YECHHE my mind screamed! The women sitting around me smiled slyly and said that as per their custom, I should eat off the half eaten plate of my husband. I could feel my cheeks going a flaming red and if they had put his plate in front of me even in jest, I know I would have walked out of the house, straight back to the railway station. There was no way I could wriggle out of sharing the plate with my sister in law at that first meal; it disturbed me greatly

---

[74]   Sumangali – married woman with husband alive

because I was still vegetarian and could not tolerate the rest of them having a side dish of fried or curried fish which they dipped into and also into the common plate of rice and dal.

At the end of the meal I said that I could not share a plate and requested that I be given a separate plate henceforth. I was frankly disturbed to see that women were accorded a lower status in the family. I later came to know that none of the sisters were educated even up to graduation while every one of Arijit's brothers were not only post graduates like himself, but had also cleared some competitive examination like civil or banking services. While the women's status did not matter at all, in Arijit's family, his mother reigned supreme in the eyes of her sons.

On my visits to their home in the early days, except when we both managed to go out to catch a movie I would see Arijit only late in the night or early in the morning. If he was at home, from his first cup of tea to the time he decided to retire to bed, he would be in the company of his family and they never made any attempt to include me in the group. Of course, language was one barrier and the women of that region observed purdah even in the mid-1970s.

This purdah affected me the most because I was the youngest daughter in law for the first seven years of my marriage; Arijit had 6 elder brothers! I had to keep my head and face covered since there were no restrictions on the men in the family. They could walk in and out of rooms. As I remember, it was always a case of the men sitting together in the outer hall and the women usually huddled in the kitchen or one of the bedrooms. Arijit's mother seemed to nurture a fear that I would entice Arijit with my 'charm' and intelligence and turn him against them. She hardly ever smiled and wore a sad, mournful expression all the time.

Within a month of our getting married, his younger brother wrote me a long letter in which he waxed eloquent about their mother and how much they all loved her and he would not tolerate anyone disrespecting her or turning her sons against her. I remember being highly offended by this letter and mentioning to Arijit that it was very impolite of his brother to write a letter like that to a total stranger. I also told Arijit that I had married a person and not a family. I realized a few years later that this belief of marrying a person was another myth of mine, because in India, a woman does marry a family.

I realized also that I was being obtuse in not recollecting that Amma had married a family and so had my sister Asha. It seemed a stupid idea at that point of time but when I thought about it some years later, there was some justification in the family's fears since it depended on Arijit's salary to quite a great extent and if I so desired I could have kept a tight hold over Arijit's money. The fact is that never during the period I lived with him had I asked him what his income was or what he was doing with it.

My first visit to Arijit's hometown was traumatic and from then on, I preferred Arijit coming to visit me in Kalingapatnam rather than my going to Bhubaneswar or Cuttack. Amma got along very well with him and Rima, and we used to have free, relaxed conversations. Otherwise our jobs took up our time. I neither had the sole responsibility of keeping him engaged nor was I hampered by rituals, restrictions and customs. Realising that my third posting was due to come up in a few months, I applied for an inter Circle transfer on the plea that my spouse was posted in Bengal circle. From the look that the branch manager gave me I knew it was a vain attempt.

It was a wonderful time for me in Kalingapatnam. The house was lovely, Amma was there taking care of all of us and we did not have any men hanging around us, except for the occasional visits from Arijit. Rima and I enjoyed going to the beach in the evenings if we returned early from work. One experience even now sends shivers down my spine when I recall it. It was a full moon evening, and while there was still enough light Rima and I went to the beach. We stood allowing the waves to splash our feet and trickle back. I don't know what happened but laughing and enjoying the cold water, we went deeper into the beach and could feel ourselves losing hold of the sand under our feet.

In the background we heard a fisherman warning us to come back, the tide was high, but before we knew it we had lost our balance and fallen. We were getting washed into the waves. The next thing I knew, we were pulled back by a couple of fishermen on either side and we lay on the sand barely able to breathe, in total shock. The fishermen slowly got us to our feet and explained that during full moon there is high tide and one should not go into the water. Nervously holding onto each other Rima and I walked back home, wet and shivering. Amma and Sasmita had been wondering where we had gone. Once we were home safe and sound, we narrated our experience, and all four of us sat and had a good cry over the narrow escape from death.

Amma always said that the period she enjoyed most was when she with us in Kalingapatnam. She managed the home, and was free to go where she wanted. Whenever we had a holiday, she would take off on her own to visit some nearby tourist spot or temple. She was a rare woman even when compared to women of this day and age, because she did not depend on someone else to entertain her; as far as I can remember from my childhood days, if she felt like seeing a Hindi film, she would just set off on her own to catch the matinee show. In fact Amma and her friends used to go to movies halls to see the 11 a.m. shows of Tamil and Telugu films! Appa and she would take in a late night show of an English movie maybe once a month and I felt proud watching them both getting into the Morris Minor and driving off.

Arijit visited me every alternate month and his short stay was a mixture of pleasure and tension for me. I seem to have got pregnant a few months after marriage and this was something that affected my health, career and my life on the whole. Everything changed completely, for the worse. Since I had a history of kidney illness and rheumatic heart, my pregnancy resulted in a recurrence of nephritis. I was not aware of what was wrong with me but was getting very tired and breathless on walking even short distances. My brother Kavi telephoned a physician he knew in Kalingapatnam and advised me to see him. I went for a checkup and was asked to get some medical tests done. The doctor said there was clear indication of my kidneys and heart being affected and he advised immediate hospitalization. I told Amma I did not want to get into a hospital in Kalingapatnam. She made telephone calls home, which were very complicated and slow given the status of telecommunications in the early 1970s. She spoke with Appa and Asha and it was arranged that I be taken on a stretcher and put on a flight bound for Hyderabad. Amma took a train the same evening. We could not afford the cost of two flight tickets.

Arijit did not know of all these developments since Amma was so busy organizing my removal to Hyderabad that she did not have time to try and inform him. He took great offence at this saying that I should have insisted that I would go to him – he told me this when he visited me almost two months after my near scrape with death; how he expected that I would have so much confidence in him puzzled me. In any case Asha took me to her home when I arrived in Hyderabad and the doctor who came to see me said that I was pregnant and I would in the normal course miscarry since I was too weak, but in case it did not happen I would have to terminate the pregnancy. I did miscarry and as it was too early a stage, it did not really upset me. My greatest despair was that I had messed up my career. The other nagging worry was Arijit's attitude to our marriage.

The doctor diagnosed that my tonsils were a source of sepsis and infection so I had to undergo a tonsillectomy. This is usually a minor surgery. But for some reason I was wheeled into the operation theatre. I did not emerge till over 2 hours. There was an emergency and the late Dr. Chari, a senior cardiologist was called in; I really don't know what it was but my heart it seems almost collapsed. Everyone was tense and my sister telephoned Arijit to inform him about my condition. My blood pressure was very high and I was kept in the hospital for a few days I think and then moved to Appa's home where for several days I lay flat and was gently raised just enough to have some soup. I was on heavy medication and put on to long acting penicillin injections to be taken every fortnight.

My family was very shocked that Arijit neither telephoned nor landed up despite being apprised of my health condition. When I think back, he probably did not know how to react because he did not bargain for all these problems when he married me. He probably did not care enough to be concerned and responsible; I really have no clue as to the reasons. He took his own time visiting me and coincided his visit with the Phase 2 Orientation & Training he had been deputed to attend. This was also residential and took place at the Training College in Shaikpet, Hyderabad. He arrived a few days earlier by which time I was shifted to my sister's house in Appuguda, Hyderabad. When Arijit arrived, he stayed with me. I secretly hoped that he would go and stay at the training college. Knowing his habits and timings it made me very awkward to burden ourselves on my sister's family. She and her family loved me very much but I felt that I was imposing Arijit on them. He never made any attempt to be courteous to them and the worst mistake he made was to ridicule me in front of them. None of my family could take this kind of ridicule.

The same group of officers who had attended the Orientation Course with me came for this training too and many of them were married. Some of them came to see me, but I wished they had not. If I had been well I would also have been part of the team. I did not have the patience or politeness to make conversation with them and felt totally out of the loop with them. I felt lost, inadequate and too exhausted. I did not know what to talk about with them. What would I have said about my illness, how would I hide my unhappiness at my own marriage, how could I expect them to understand how it pained me that in the office I was considered substandard? Was all this a consequence of one personal decision? What a price I was having to pay!

Arijit was once again obsessed with the crazy suspicion that I was in love with someone else. I wished to be left alone with my family. In my mind, my family did not include him. Every single day of the four weeks he was with me was a nightmare for me. However I decided to return with him to Bhubaneswar though everyone in the family was against it. We took a flight and Appa sent the luggage by train. Arijit had not been allotted a house as yet and so we stayed with his brother, Ranveer. We were given the living room and as was common in those days, we slept on a thin mat on the floor. During the day I had to move to the kitchen or some other room where Ranveer did not come. His wife had just had her first baby and was pretty hassled since I did not know how to cook. She was a Hindi teacher in the Government High School in Bhubaneswar and leaving the baby with a boy to mind it she quickly cooked a basic meal and rushed off to work. Breakfast was bread and jam for me. The lunch consisted of boiled rice, a watery dal and two thin slices of fried brinjal. A bit of salt and green chillis were always served. Arijit could see that this was not enough nutrition for me and in the evenings he would take me out in a rickshaw and buy masala dosa for me to eat while the rickshaw took us round the town. Since there was no privacy in the house we also used to do our hugging and kissing on the rickshaw ride, with the plastic curtain drawn in front so as to hide us from the public eye! He was very affectionate and physically attracted but suddenly something would happen that would send him on a trip of grim suspicion about my affection for him.

For example when he landed up to visit me in Hyderabad during my illness, he brought all the clothes I had left in his house in Cuttack, bristling with irritation, the cause of which I could not fathom. He told me many years later that his younger sister was actually hiring out my expensive silk saris to friends and neighbors; it sounded so weird to me! Lying in bed during that illness, I realized my mistake in hastening into a relationship without getting to know anything about the other person in terms of family background, culture and habits, language and dialect, food preferences. Neither of us thought about all these things. I also did not realize that there are clear cut rules for men and women in his social set up. Yes, there were several instances of wife beating that I witnessed in my family and society, but we did not have any taboos that I considered weird. Till my marriage I had not been exposed to unspoken rules of how women should behave. My family had only imposed one rule before marriage - I could not go partying, or date boys, but the same rule applied to my brother too. There was never any restriction on my talking with boys or men.

The restrictions I encountered when I entered my marital home disturbed me. Arijit's jealousy and insecurity were additional tensions I could not fathom. I understood the mistake we both made. We had been impulsive rushing into a marriage to start with and did not take any pains later on, to set right the casualness with which we had entered into what is called a lifetime relationship.

Any man/woman relationship that is more than casual needs both partners to really put in an effort to make it work. But the common perception is that this is a problem women have to resolve. I realized this only after I married. *I* felt the pain and so *I* had to deal with it. Arijit as the man was not even conscious that the relationship needed to be worked on. I had to see how to overcome my discomfiture with his family and culture and also ensure that he did not encounter any inconvenience when he was with my family. Arijit's attitude was that I should fall into the correct slot, if life after marriage appeared to be a jigsaw puzzle. It was my problem and I had to find my place.

Arijit's casualness when I was recuperating hurt me. Even after I joined him in Bhubaneswar I had to continue taking the long acting Penicillin injections at fortnightly intervals. His elder brother Ranveer found a compounder[75] who was prepared to administer the injection once every fortnight. I dreaded every injection but Arijit was strangely not affected or seemed not to be affected by my tension. It was Ranveer who showed concern, but I could not talk with him since he was my elder brother in law.

A month later we found a house which had four apartments and the other three were also occupied by bank officers. The apartment was very nice and spacious and it actually had a

---

[75]   Compounder – assistant to medical practitioners in their clinics

master bedroom. What luxury, I thought. Thatha came to visit with a bag of rice, kerosene, sugar, dal and oil. He occupied the guest bedroom and it was such a blessing to have him around. He would be up early in the morning and I just had to leave the vegetables on the dining table for him to chop up just the size and shape I wanted. Somehow through trial and error I was able to cook the basic dal, rice and vegetable. I learnt to make an omelet.

There was a slum comprising of Telugu speaking migrants and I got myself a wonderful housemaid. Armed with Saramma my housemaid I felt I could conquer the world. Her husband was a rickshaw driver and my life was made since I had to just send word to him whenever I wanted to go out; the battered cycle rickshaw felt like a Chevrolet when I went round town in it! Thatha and I would go to the weekly market and buy vegetables. Since I was not exposed to non-vegetarian food Arijit had to restrict himself to eating vegetables only in the initial months. Even the vegetables we ate were very different and it amused me that he had to have potatoes in every dish at every meal.

Whenever Thatha visited, he stayed for at least a month and would help me with some of the household chores. Observing this and the relief it gave me, Arijit came in to help after Thatha's departure. It was fun that both of us sat on the floor and picked rice or he chopped vegetables and peeled potatoes while I fried something. The front door would usually be kept ajar since it was quite safe and one of us did not have to go and answer the door every time there was a visitor.

The lady upstairs decided to visit me for something and came in so silently that we did not even hear her. She even walked out as silently and later, when she made fun of me, saying that I had Arijitbabu' under my thumb, I asked what she meant and she said she dropped in a couple of days back and saw that I made him help in the kitchen. This became a topic of conversation between her husband and her and thereon it was obviously repeated as a joke in his office and Arijit suddenly took to sitting with his morning cup of tea, face buried behind a newspaper, disappearing into the bathroom without his usual shout that he was going, and then waiting at the table for his breakfast.

The stiff upper lip attitude puzzled me. In the early days he would actually come home for lunch but slowly he was weaned away from the routine by his colleagues. Suddenly he would come and say we're going for a movie tonight and if I asked why, he would say that the neighbours had planned it and so we go. This kind of arbitrary decision bothered me because I had to wake up early in the mornings on week days; my refusal would put him in a bad mood and so I accompanied them quietly.

As time went on, I slowly started becoming quieter and working mechanically. I was still on sick leave and kept extending it by providing medical certificates issued by the bank certified doctor. Once it so happened that I delayed submitting my leave extension letter and since I was on probation, I was sent a summons to be present for a hearing at the Regional Office in Hyderabad. I went and committed what one would call a 'hara kiri.'

The Chairman, deputy director and personnel manager (who hated me) were on the panel and I was sitting opposite them alone. I was questioned if I was really sick and I said that I could give them the names of the doctors in the city who were treating me and they could verify right at that moment. They ignored my statement and said that it was time I reported for my third posting in Guntur. I asked why they could not consider my request for an inter circle transfer. They said such transfers are not easy and I said, 'Unless one's father is a senior officer in the same bank, like 'Mrs. X'. They could not believe that I had actually said it. The Chairman gave a half smile and pitifully shook his head. The personnel manager glared and almost had a fit. I knew I had messed up my chance of getting back to work in the bank. They walked out and the deputy director came back and asked me why I had spoken the way I had and I asked if truth was insubordination. He said that I still had a chance if I apologized to the personnel manager, withdrew my transfer request and gave a firm date for joining duty in Guntur. I refused to do any of it. He asked if I would like to resign and I said 'No, I want my security deposit back so you can throw me out.' Thus ended the saga of my first ever job and career.

I returned to Bhubaneswar and got down to preparing for my Masters final examinations which was still incomplete. This preparation was so different from the kind of discipline I was used to. Here, suddenly Arijit's sister in law decided to come and stay at our place with her infant daughter. I had no say in the matter. The baby had an attack of diarrhea and I was cleaning up the mess. The mother was asking me, 'Usha, why is the baby's stool green and smelly?' It was as if I had borne and brought up a dozen babies or was a pediatrician! It irritated me and I said that she should probably stop eating so much of fatty meat since she was breastfeeding.

To be honest, I was unconsciously giving expression to my unease at the way she kept eating a lot of fatty meat. Somehow, the sight of a person eating large quantities of meat was repugnant to me. Though I did start eating meat and fish slowly, my comfort food was only vegetarian. I waited for her to shift to her husband's house and was ever so relieved when she finally did. She was a bossy type of person and had a way of simply giving instructions that had to be followed – it may be a trait she cultivated once her husband became a police officer. She was younger than me in age but senior in hierarchy and as a result, even after she moved out I was expected to visit her almost every day. She had a platoon of constables at her service.

I suggested that Arijit's father move in to her home so that my housework would be reduced and I could pay more attention to my studies. It was made into a big issue where her husband intervened and said something about his father not being an orphan and I was not doing a favour looking after him, I was doing my duty. Learning fast, I just did not rise to the bait and simply focused on my studies. I was instinctively beginning to understand patriarchy! Arijit thankfully understood my stance and did not interfere.

Cooking, ironing Arijit's clothes, supervising the housemaid's work, providing sex and emotional cushioning for a spouse, while preparing for my Masters examinations was not easy. Just a day before I was to leave for Hyderabad, Arijit's sister in law sent word that she wanted me to prepare 40 potato cutlets for her evening's get together. I quietly prepared and dispatched the whole lot. Arijit was surprised at what I had done and asked why I took on the task when I had my own preoccupation. I had the good sense not to retort sharply. I had come to realise that a husband's affections to his siblings and family are unpredictable and unquestionable.

My performance in the examinations was not as good as the first year but still good. I returned after about 15 days, arrived at the railway station and took a cycle rickshaw home to my 'still in bed' husband. He was pleased to see me and made a pretense of getting me a cup of coffee. I freshened up and sat on the bed; for some reason I bent forward to pick up something from the floor. I was shocked to see that under the cot were around 15 unwashed teacups and stacks of daily newspapers. I asked Saramma why she had left them under the cot and she said that 'Babugaru[76]' never allowed her to clean the room. I asked 'What's going on?' and he said 'This will teach you not to ever leave me and go away.' If he thought I would see it as an expression of undying love and was floored by it he was mistaken.

My stupidity was that I actually expected him to perceive and read my irritation! I existed for him in a very peculiar way – he loved me and that was a given, about which I should not expect a demonstration or reassurance; there were certain expectations I would fulfill, as far as he, his family and friends were concerned, but he did not have any obligations towards my family. He provided me food, shelter and entertainment and I had opted to give up my career so what did I have to complain about. Too tired to argue, I adjusted to the routine and tried to make the best of the situation.

The two ladies in the adjacent apartments both had teaching jobs in a nearby women's college and so they would leave in the morning and return at 3 or 4 p.m. Once they came home they were busy with their respective babies so there was not much talking that we did except across the common courtyard adjoining the kitchen. The lady living on top of our apartment had four kids and she was a loquacious person. I visited her pretty often till one day she repeated a nasty joke that her husband seemed to have related about Arijit. It seems that they all ragged him because we did not have any kids saying Arijit was only spilling gas into me.

It was around this time that Arijit had started changing. I said that it was still not all that late; we could still have a child. I was just about recovering and had finished my Masters so what's the hurry. This is when I learnt what peer

---

[76]   Babugaru – Master of the house

pressure among men is. I also realized with time that this has a very strong effect on them and is largely responsible for their attitude and behavior towards women and girls.

I noticed that whenever any of Arijit's friends visited our home, his tone to me would change. It was a kind of bossy, careless one where even the visitors felt awkward. I would bring in the tea and if I made an attempt to sit with them he would give me an obtuse look which indicated that I leave the room. I was expected to supply endless cups of tea even at 10 or 11 p.m. If it was raining he expected me to fry some snacks. They all started having their parties at our home since none of the others could dare to serve liquor in their homes.

He did not like my family visiting me since that would curtail his parties. I realized that I did not fit the definition of 'wife.' Devotion, passive acceptance, 'one step behind,' and playing hostess all the time were not my style. I also realized by then that what was generally seen as a successful relationship was where one partner, usually the wife, is passive. I was not a passive personality certainly and Arijit's assumption was that by virtue of his birth he was the active partner.

If I complained, he would claim that he never stopped me from being active. Certainly he never told me that I should or should not do something. He did not care to see the change that my personality underwent subsequent to our marriage. He preened himself that he was unique for having found a wife like me!

How did love and marriage change me so drastically where my one and only concern was whether my husband was smiling, that he got the perfect cup of tea at the right time, that his bath water was just about the right temperature, that his bed was made while he was in his bath, so that when he came out he could see a neat and tidy room. Did he say it was his expectation ... no, I observed the smug smile of satisfaction on his face and concluded that I should keep clutter out of his sight. I, who had not done a spot of housework before marriage was ironing everything from his clothes to the bed linen and handkerchiefs. We had not got a gas connection and I had to cook on a stove using sawdust as fuel. I still remember the heat blisters I got on my waist. If I mentioned it he would ask, 'Who asked you to do it? I would have brought something for us to eat.' But at a later point in time, when he looked at me while counting his money and said we need to spend carefully, how could I not have felt guilty? This is not only Arijit I am talking about; I guess it applies for almost all the men I have come across. Speaking for myself, love between two persons of the opposite sex and marriage as its natural consequence has done me inexpressible damage.

I lost my sunny smile, carefree laughter, easy way of mingling with people. It was inevitable, I suppose, with a husband who suspected that I was in love with every man from the milkman or the vegetable vendor to one or other of his colleagues just because I laughed or smiled with them. When I asked Arijit why he was so suspicious he laughingly replied that I should be happy to have such a possessive husband! I did not feel proud… I felt drained trying to keep him free of suspicion and in good humor all the time.

My family members used to visit me regularly since they were worried about my health. I just recovered from the kidney problem and landed up with an attack of appendicitis. I sent a telegram to Appa about it and he asked me to take the first train and come to Hyderabad for a checkup. I went and was advised to have it removed. It was again hospitalization and surgery and I am glad Arijit accompanied me.

On our return he mumbled something about my becoming a burden on him. This puzzled and hurt me because I saw that healthwise, I was a burden on my family right from birth and it was never a source of irritation or nastiness. It was not a condition I enjoyed but there was nothing I could do. It was therefore an unsettling revelation that my husband did not like being saddled with a sickly wife. I felt that he could have prevented getting saddled with a sickly person by doing adequate research on me and my health, financial and overall status before marrying me; he undoubtedly rushed into the marriage, whatever the reason may have been. I cannot ascribe such immense persuasive powers to myself that I could have made him marry me against his wishes. The regret that I was a physically frail person was nevertheless very strongly felt by him and his family.

Throughout my stay in Bhubaneswar his father would stay with us for long spells of time since I did not indulge in any kind of idle talk and also ensured that he got his tea and meals on time. When Arijit was promoted as manager he was entitled to better living quarters. For this we had to move house. It was a bigger house and I was happy because I had a family from Karnataka for my neighbours; this family occupied one portion and the house owners lived in the other portion of the ground floor. They had a love for gardening and the front and back yards were lush with herbal and fruit trees, plants, exotic creepers and flowers. It was in this house that I first saw a cashew tree and a cinnamon tree. It was such pleasure being able to just peel a bit of fresh green cinnamon bark or a leaf to add to my curries or spiced rice. Cashew fruit was such a seasonal rarity in Hyderabad and here with a *tree bearing the fruit*, I loved plucking them and making sambar just like Amma used to. Of course, not everyone likes the sweet, tangy taste and most often only I would be eating it. We were always given papayas, mangoes, lemons and fresh coconuts by our house owners.

I recall Bhubaneswar as a city where I was able to connect to nature in a special way. The neighbor had a cow and I found it fascinating to watch the calving process; I marveled at the way the cow licked her calf clean and the little one slowly crouched, straightened, hobbled onto its feet and then in no time at all started frolicking round the yard. The vegetable market was within walking distance and on many occasions I would find a peacock and hen mating right in the middle of the street! Arijit's father would so often point out rare birds perched on a nearby tree.

We had huge snakes wending their way into a well in our backyard. Sometimes we would find snakeskins on the path. I was busy in the kitchen one day and looked up to find Arijit at the door. I was about to step back in greeting when he cautioned me not to move. He then gingerly held me and brought me forward, out of the kitchen. He then pointed to what I would have stepped on to – a pair of scorpions were mating! It was the only time I have ever seen scorpions in the act. Those were the days when one could count the number of cars in Bhubaneswar!

For the first two months of shifting into the new house Arijit would leave for office early in the morning and joined me at home for lunch. Later on he slipped into leaving late and though his office was not too far away he stopped coming home for lunch. Not only that, he started arriving home very late in the evenings. When he did come home he would be quite drunk and could barely manage to control his scooter. One evening it was past midnight and I was worried.

I got into a rickshaw to search for him. I went to his office and was told that he had just left. On my way back I found him on the scooter. He was totally drunk and barely managing to keep the scooter balanced. He managed to bring the scooter in and park it after allowing it to drop once. The house owner and the neighbours were all standing outside. They said that he should be ashamed for making me so anxious, but he was not

sobre enough to even comprehend that they were talking to him.
I had to help him up the stairs. He fell flat on the floor in the
dining hall and threw up. I washed him and dragged him to the
bedroom and helped him on to the bed and then cleaned up the
mess he had made in the dining hall. I slept in the guest room.

I was reaching my peak of unrest and started withdrawing
into myself. We hardly exchanged any words. I also discovered
that he had got addicted to drinking cough syrups; these were
common enough addictions among many people I guess
but my exposure to such happenings was zero and therefore
incomprehensible when they surfaced in someone close to me.
His dinner time kept getting later and I got into the habit of
eating early and retiring to bed. He withdrew into longer spells
of silence and I had lost my will to keep alive a conversation.
Mechanically I always ensured that his meals were laid out for
him to eat whenever he pleased.

I was not told that I was a problem but the behavior and
body language of my husband and his family conveyed this
to me. I went through several gynecological tests to diagnose
why I was not getting pregnant. Nobody understood that
I had been very sick for such a long time and maybe that
had some effect. I would go alone to the nursing home for
the various tests. One tube patency test where the fallopian
tubes and uterus are injected with a mixture of cortisone,
streptomycin and penicillin resulted in a severe allergy where
my entire uterus and tubes were itching. I was going crazy
and scratching my skin. I asked Arijit to call the doctor. He
telephoned the doctor and she said that it must have been
sensitivity to streptomycin and the duty doctor of the nursing
home came and gave me the antihistamine intravenously.

I noticed another strange behavior in Arijit during the
times that I was unwell. He would just move out of the room
leaving me alone. He would stand outside smoking even

though I would weakly call out to him because I wanted to feel comforted with his presence. This was totally in contrast to what I did when he was sick. I would try to keep him as comfortable as possible, sitting by him, cooling his fever with cold compresses, washing his head with cold water in order to bring down his temperature.

When I asked him he wryly said that he did not like to see me sick. I laughed that I was sicker than well in my life and would probably continue to be so even later and what was he going to do. He said that if he had known this earlier he would not have married me. He had obviously planned that our joint income would give us a comfortable life and instead he was being burdened with an unemployed, sick wife whose medical expenses he had to bear.

His younger brother got married and there was so much tension in the family that I had still not borne a child. His mother came to live with us. She tied a 'taveez[77]' onto my upper arm and made me drink some milk into which she had mixed some strange stuff. She also instructed that I sleep on the bare floor for 7 days and not allow Arijit to come near me. After this, she said, I would certainly get pregnant. She had instructed that her youngest son delay having a child till such time that I had a child! By this time I had lost all patience. I wanted to quit but where would I go, was my dilemma. I was out of touch with any kind of office work. I knew I could not stay on in the same town and live alone – how would I survive. I then planned to leave for Calcutta and find a job as a housemaid. A post graduate in Economics, a state ranker

---

[77]   Taveez – a black string with a coin or bead believed to ward off evil spirits

at the graduation level, finding herself fit only to work as a housemaid!

Around the same time, my sister Asha seemed to have intuitively felt my despair. She telephoned and said that her friend were coming on a holiday to Bhubaneswar and could I put them up for a couple of days. It was one of those times when I was firm with Arijit. He shifted his father and sister to his brother's house for a week and prepared for the visit of these people who became my saviors in one sense. I would not be sitting and writing this but for them. By the time of their visit, I had made up my mind to leave Arijit. Where do I go was the question. Considering that it was the first time we were meeting, the friend could not say much to me but she just said that Asha was worried to death about me. Suddenly I knew what to do.

When they were leaving they asked me when are we seeing you in Hyderabad and I just said January 17th. It was exactly a month away. They smiled and asked, 'Sure?' I nodded. After they left, I telephoned my sister and asked her to immediately send me Rs.100 by telegraphic money order. As soon as the money arrived, I went to the railway station and booked myself a ticket to leave on 16th January 1979. Arijit's mother and sister were living with us and so I was very careful in packing for my departure. About 10 days before my departure I told him that I was going to Hyderabad since I felt like a change. He mumbled about not getting tickets and I said I would manage that. I did not tell him that the ticket was already with me. His mother was somehow sensing something was amiss and asked why both of us could not go at a later date and what will he do. I replied that she was there and it should not be a problem. She noticed how carefully I was packing all my clothes and kept asking why I needed so much for 10 days. I simply smiled and moved away.

On the day of my departure, Arijit as expected, did not bother to turn up even for lunch, but I organized a rickshaw to carry me and my baggage to the railway station. His mother was standing at the top of the stairs with tears streaming down her cheeks and his sister was also looking worried and unsettled. The rickshaw puller parked his vehicle and came with me to my compartment. He placed my suitcase under the seat and touched my feet and with tears in his eyes, said, 'Ammagaru, you are Lakshmi, we will never forget you, travel safe.' I felt sad then, but nervous for the train to pull out of the platform. Just two minutes before its departure Arijit came bounding in and said that I should have waited for him. I smiled wryly and he said 'You'll come back like a bad penny... who will keep you there? Your father is an alcoholic and your brother has his family as has your sister. You don't have anyone but me.' The train started moving and he shouted that I should return in 10 days' time and jumped off. The train picked up speed and my heart regained its normal rhythm. I was so nervous when Arijit came on to the train that I had almost stopped breathing. I had already sent a telegram to my sister about my arrival and so when the train reached Hyderabad railway station I looked out and found my sister, her husband and the friend who came to Bhubaneswar. I must have looked terrible because Asha, my sister seemed to be fighting to keep her tears under control. Once I got off the train she asked me if I wanted to go to Amma or with her and I said I wanted to be with her. It was such a strange feeling that I seemed to have lost my voice.

Everything was hazy and I just allowed myself to be taken inside the house and when the bath water was ready I went in for my bath. That feeling of total paralysis is something indescribable. I could not do the simplest of things – I could not decide whether I wanted a glass of water or not. Asha served me some food, I ate. She asked if I wanted to rest, I lay on a bed and curled up into a fetal position. I told her that I didn't want to meet my parents or any other family members just then and she quietly nodded. I would lie in bed all night with her two girls, my eyes wide open. It was the time just after the Emergency was lifted in India and there was an Enquiry Commission set up to look into the excesses of the state.

In Andhra Pradesh, the Commission hearing was going on and Rajamama was a legal counsel on the panel. Every day there would be people walking in, discussions, eating together, laughing together and in the midst of all this Asha never lost her sight of me and Rajamama always had the time and presence of mind to pat my head and say not to worry, things will work out. Their concern and attention towards me, just an individual with a very silly problem is something that I will never forget as long as I live. They gave me yet another lease on life.

Earlier it was physical health problems that I battled with. But in 1979 I was an emotionally, intellectually broken creature with no sense of self-worth. My family helped me build it up slowly, never hurrying me, never making me feel unwanted. After three weeks or so, Arijit called up Appa and coming to know that I was with Asha, he did not call but wrote me a long letter instead. I realized at this time what it is to lie in bed with eyes wide open, staring into a darkness which stared back at me. It took a lot of effort to convince myself that my eyelids could and should blink, that my mind should start thinking and that my voice should start being heard. Very gently Asha suggested that I think of keeping myself occupied; my interest was only in academics. Armed with references from Asha's wonderful friends, I went to the Staff College in Hyderabad to enquire about procedures for getting admission for an MPhil course. I went to meet a professor there and he started talking with me and I was nervous, hesitant, then he asked me what I had been doing in the past year. I replied that I was a housewife. He suddenly said, "I don't understand why you housewives can't be satisfied with what you do, why can't you just be happy minding your homes, why do you come to us with fancy notions of getting into academics?' I somehow kept a straight face, left the place and on arriving at Asha's place, sat down on the bed trying to get myself under control. Asha came in and asked how the meeting went and I burst into tears, sobbing loudly. Rajamama heard me and came in and asked 'did that … misbehave with you? I knew he was no good…' I realized that they both thought that I was subjected to some kind of sexual advances. This set me off laughing and I reassured them that it was nothing of that sort. This was the point of time when I broke out of the trauma.

With renewed determination, I started scanning the newspapers every day for some job opening. I had decided that I would not block my mind to any kind of job. I found an opening as an assistant in a printing press in Hyderabad. On reaching the address given in the newspaper, I found it was a medium sized garage converted into an office. I went up the steps and found a bespectacled young man behind a heap of printed paper and he asked what I wanted. I said I came in response to the newspaper advertisement. His head shot out of the heap and he asked if I was really interested in the job. I said I was. He said I would need to attend to the telephone, take printing orders, get the layout done by the printer, read the proofs, make necessary corrections, get the final printing done and then write the bill, ensure order delivery and payment collection. I knew nothing about printing, was getting into a job after a break of six years and was so excited that the only question I asked was where I should sit. The proprietor was bemused and asked if I did not want to know what my salary would be and I said of course, but he took advantage of the situation and said he could only pay me Rs.150 per month. A beginning had to be made and I had no choice so I agreed and started work the same day. In 1979 the letterpress printing was popular. Normally printing houses would invest only in the necessary equipment and one or two workers who could either learn the technique or already knew it. The salaries were also low.

In this printing press where I had started working, there was a fairly elderly man who handled the machine and the proprietor undertook the delivery. There was one chair with matching table and one smaller table with a stool. It was only when the proprietor went out that I could sit on the chair. The worse problem was that there was no toilet. I would control myself from 11 a.m. till I reached home around 6.30 p.m. There were no public toilets and no friend, acquaintance or relative living nearby. I had to change two buses to come from Asha's home. When I had my periods I would stay home on the second day, because it would have been impossible to manage without a toilet. Despite the problems it was a job I thoroughly enjoyed.

Letterpress printing was yet another skill I learnt and very quickly I managed to actually compose full pages. Of course, at the end of the day my fingertips would be heavily stained with ink which was difficult to rub off, but the excitement of placing letters in order, seeing words form and sentences leaping out of the frame, how can I describe it? The job of printing each frame on to the paper was undertaken by the 'printer uncle.' We would allow the ink to dry and towards the end of the day, cut the paper to the specified size. We mainly took orders for invitation cards, pamphlets and circulars with basic style. We had quite a good business and after a month, I discovered that the proprietor used to also run a fortnightly magazine earlier. I asked why we don't try to revive that. He showed an old copy and explained that it involved collecting content, getting advertisements and also having a fairly good circulation. I gamely took on the challenge and while on paper, the proprietor was the editor, I was writer, editor, printer, proof reader, publicity manager, all rolled into one!

I completely changed the content to suit what I could manage. One major feature article, three small write ups, a small health tips column, what your stars foretell column, the editor's column and one or two advertisements. I had to plan my day carefully in order to meet the deadline. The contacts of my family, my friends circle, all proved to be very useful. They brought me advertisements and content for the feature article. I would fish out some health tip from my grandmothers' home remedies. The fortune telling was quite a hit and a big joke as well; the way I wrote this column was that I would listen to my family's or friend's hopes and disappointments during casual conversations and then prepare the contents of my 'what the stars foretell' column on that. These same people, who normally had a healthy disbelief in such fortune telling, I found, started turning the magazine pages to read this column! They would also casually say that the column was predicting pretty accurately! I did not let on as to what I was doing till almost a year later.

I was so absorbed in my work that I did not think about the financial part of it at all till one day my brother Kavi asked as to how much I was getting as commission for the advertisements. The next day, while calculating the income from the magazine with the proprietor I asked what he was going to pay me as commission for the advertisements. He was taken aback but quickly hid it and asked what I expected, so I said I should get 30% of the advertisement cost. He bargained and we settled at 20%. This gave me an impetus to collect more advertisements since I was getting additional money. The task of getting advertisements was a tough one since companies were not so many in those days and I had to travel round the city quite a bit in order to meet with company heads (who were all men), deal with the usual attempts to make physical contact, make excuses for not going on dates, getting the advertisement and finally the cheque. Nevertheless, it was a fascinating phase in my life.

In order to save money I would try and walk as much distance as possible. Every bit saved mattered. I was still staying with Asha and one of her friends said that there was an opening for a teacher in a reputed boys' school and would I be interested. I decided to take on the job though the salary was almost the same as what I was drawing in the press. The shift was because I felt it would give me status, did not involve running around the city the whole day, would provide me clean sitting and toilet facilities and had the potential of helping me get into the academic line. My boss at the press acknowledged that he benefited from my service with him because I had revived the magazine which he had started with a passion.

Teaching in a boys' school was fun. I was asked to teach English and Moral Science from Class 6 to Class 10; Moral Science was only till Class 7 and so it was essentially English. Except for two or three women teachers, I did not mingle with anybody else. The experience was so different from what I had known during my student days. This school itself was only for the elite sections of society and most of us teachers did not hail from the same class. This posed endless problems since the 'whiling away time' boys were a distraction for the whole class and if any of us tried to censure any of them we would be told that his father or grandfather was on the school board and he would see how we continue to keep our job. Some of us would be most crassly told by an errant student, "I know how to tackle you..."

The 'class' difference between some of us teachers and the students was so obvious; most of the teachers hailed from the middle class and practically all the students, given the fact that it was an exclusive school, were from the 'upper class.' This showed up in the way we commuted; we teachers commuted by bus while most of the students had their swanky cars coming in and picking them up when school gave over. The job was temporary and I was not assured that the contract would be renewed. The uncertainty was too much for me to bear and when Rajamama said that the local office of Indi Am Airlines was looking for a counter assistant and he could put in a reference, I jumped into that.

I went into yet another area of work in which I had no experience at all. It was called Ratlam Travels and was the General Sales Agency of Indi Am Airlines for south India. The managing director was based in Madras and he was a client of Rajamama. The office, which comprised a fairly large sized hall had two partitions - one each for the accounts department and the manager's cabin. It was on the ground floor of a building in Appuguda, a busy area surrounded by travel agencies. I was asked to report to the manager who was staying in a hotel in Hyderabad. He expected me to go into his room but I stayed in the lobby and he came to interview me. I immediately saw that he was a heavy drinker and wondered how I would deal with it. There was not much choice except to try it out.

Fortunately it turned out that he was leaving for some job in Saudi Arabia and there was another wonderful man who was the sales officer and who was going to be promoted as manager. He was a thorough gentleman, open hearted and full of laughter and fun. He was also very good at his work, which was sales as well as reservation and ticketing.

My first manager was a pain. He was very possessive about information and knowledge and would not share his with any of us; he was yet another example of a highly resentful male chauvinist. It was 1980 and we had the telex communication system. Our main link was with Delhi and every day we had to type the bookings that had come in and telex the same to the Delhi reservations office. The next day we would get the confirmation and convey the same to the client following which changes may be made or he/she would make the payment and our office would issue the ticket after checking the travel documents.

My colleague and I sat in the outer hall and the manager sat in one cabin while the accountant sat in another, where the telex was also kept. For the first few days I had to just sit twiddling my thumbs. Then I dared to ask the manager if he would please give me some work. He laughed or ignored me according to his mood and that was it. Our sales officer was out most of the time visiting travel agents. After a week I was given the reservation cards and asked to go through them. I did but was never allowed to fill any cards.

One day I caught the sales officer alone and told him that the manager was really behaving shabbily by not giving me any work. Then he quietly helped me fill in a reservation card. He seems to have told the manager to delegate work to me since later on I would have to look after the reservations and other documentation. I started getting work and with my colleague it was quite a fun place because she was a very jovial person. The manager seemed to like dealing with her rather than me, probably because she laughed and chatted easily.

Taking matters into my hands, I started going into the telex room when he was at work to peek over his shoulder. It was really weird because from the next day onwards he started coming in early and finishing all the telex work before

I arrived. I was bent on learning and would go through the reams of used telex paper lying on the floor in order to learn the what and how of reservations. This man would even keep the reservations and ticketing manual under lock and key. I urged my colleague to ask him for the manual and when he gave it to her we both sat and read through it and I made copious notes. Then I started coming in early in the morning. He would have arrived a half hour early and finished the telex dispatch. I persevered and he had to allow me to peek over his shoulder while he worked on the machine. I literally pleaded with him to allow me to update the reservation status on the cards based on the telex received. This man's behavior reminded me of my senior officer in National Bank who resisted teaching me how to handle transactions.

As the days progressed this manager landed up quite drunk and sometimes did not turn up at all and then he left for some country in Saudi Arabia. The sales officer was cool in letting me do the work and I must admit rather shamefully that given the limited volume of work during the early days I also behaved like my ex manager whom I cribbed so much about. I hardly gave my colleague a chance to handle the reservations. She must have felt disappointed but never let it show. She just laughed and said a day would come when both of us would find the work too much to handle and we would need a third person, which turned out to be true and another wonderful young woman joined us. It was really exciting.

I adopted a strategy, with my new boss's support. I would make reservations for the months of August and September to all popular cities in the U.S.A. as "4Reddy, or 5Rao – BOMJFK", etc. When it was peak season we had seats when even Air India could not offer any. A whole lot of bookings came to us by default and then we would use the 'change name to' tool for converting to the actual names!

The work was hectic and quite often I would work late into the evening, but when my colleague offered to help, I would say I could manage. I don't know why I was so petty and scornful of her laughter and wide smile. I was always scornful of the way she came across with male clients and visitors. The interesting part was that while she was literally inviting male attention, I was getting a whole lot of male attention. Most of it I did not like but I also had some memorable short lived love affairs during this time. I feel it was only then that I became of aware of my sexuality.

I was in my early 30s and reinforced with a new confidence, I felt adult, a person. While sex was something pretty regular throughout my seven years of married life, it was more to please my husband. With the lovers who came into my life from 1980, it was me, my pleasure and need. I had not ever longed for the feeling earlier on because I assumed that pleasure was only for the man. My sexual awakening was a wonderful gift of life.

Particularly with Pratik, I learnt to love and cherish my body, to experience a pleasure earlier unknown to me, discover what I was, and truly loved him for giving me such pleasure. It was a purely physical attraction and he drew pleasure from giving me pleasure. It was the best experience in my whole life. I met him when I decided to take evening classes to learn Spanish after my work and we drew together like magnets. From the day we set eyes on each other, there was nothing else and nobody else but the two of us. He was 10 years younger than me but nothing mattered. He was the one steady boyfriend I had for a few years and later he decided that he had to get married to someone younger, so we parted ways. After him I lost interest in the sexual aspect of life because I did not like the idea of being at the mercy of yet another man's insecurities.

Looking back, I can say that once again just as in my teens, there were several things happening simultaneously and each was totally different from the other when I entered my 30s. The foremost experience was that of getting back my self-confidence and reiterated awareness that financial independence and a career were primary for me. Among the exciting experiences, one was my exposure to skills that I had never known before like letterpress printing, composing, printing and publishing a regular magazine, telex communication and airline ticketing, learning French. As icing on the cake, I was selected to attend a week long reservations and ticketing course at the Indi Am Airlines office in London and since Amma's brother Raghu and family lived in suburban London I was persuaded to have a holiday with them after the course. And so, I went on my first ever foreign trip. I was the first in the immediate family to 'go abroad.' This is an experience I shall never forget. None of us having travelled beyond Delhi, we had no idea about the weather, dress code, etc. Asha gave me a pair of canary yellow pants and some collared blouse belonging to one of her daughters and for the rest of clothing, I carried my daily wear saris.

I went to Delhi where I stayed with one of my cousins; I felt mortified at the prospect of wearing the yellow pants, but wore them nevertheless, since I had been instructed to do so by Asha. I was escorted to the airport by my cousin and after a rushed goodbye I went and joined the snake line queue at the airport. At the ticket counter I was told that as staff I would be seated in business class. It was on this trip that I learnt that I just had to follow the queue and ask very few questions. I hung around for the boarding call after completing the formalities and I noticed that some people were looking at me quite amused while most of them studiously ignored me. The other art I learnt was that of behaving as if the person in front of me did not exist. For me this was a new and peculiarly Western type of behavior, nevertheless I adopted it.

In the aircraft I was seated next to a German in a formal black suit. Suddenly he called a stewardess and they exchanged some words in German and the chief steward was summoned and then I was asked very tentatively if I would mind changing my seat and they would seat me in first class. I understood what racism was at that time. In any case, I was quite happy to move into first class and had a jolly and drunken Frenchman seated next to me. The plush seating and leg space were wonderful except that I was too wound up to enjoy it all. I refused all the food and drink and waited for the flight to land. On landing it was wonderful because there was no need to ask any questions, so clear were the directions posted everywhere at Heathrow airport. My uncle Raghu was waiting outside and it was ever so cold. He had thoughtfully brought me a sweater and coat. His wife and I were almost the same size and I was comfortable.

I was allowed to stay with family and attend the classes. The first day, my cousin brought along a route map of the London Tube and explained it to me. He marked out where I should get off and the route to walk to the training center. That trip is a memorable one. Once the training got over, I accompanied my aunt for a couple of days on her shopping sprees and enjoyed walking through Marks & Spencer's, where people like us went and we also ventured into some of the really high end shops like Harrods, where I saw the extreme politeness with which the English disguise their contempt for you! My dress and walk obviously showed me to be a poor Asian visitor with neither the taste nor the money to be their customer. Nothing fazed me – I was a visitor, and absorbed as much of the city as I could. One day Raghu uncle took me to Kew Gardens and Trafalgar Square. The garden was lovely and the verdant greenness of the place is a memory I awaken every time I want to cheer myself up even now.

What I found interesting and also awkward (since I was with my uncle) was the physical intimacy men and women engaged in publicly. On the next day I went alone to wander around the parks and streets and just keep crisscrossing around in the underground tube. Before returning to my uncle's I went to Totten ham Court Road and booked two tours at the tour operator's for myself – one was a city tour and the other was to Stratford on Avon. I had decided to see as much as possible since I was so familiar with England by way of books. Both the tours were enthralling for me. One very interesting experience I have always remembered is that of my lunch. The tours included lunch and for the city tour we were taken to a restaurant; I asked for a vegetarian lunch in which I got bread, butter, cheese and a salad, ending with a pastry and coffee. The serving was really huge and I could only eat a bit of it. I was pushing off the uneaten dish to a side. Suddenly a lady sitting opposite, who had been observing me asked if I had finished eating and I said yes, then she asked if I minded her finishing the leftovers. I was surprised and nodded. She asked me again and I had to say yes. Then she quickly polished off the food. Immediately after that she completely ignored me. Just towards the end of the tour she came up and asked me if I was taking any other tour and I said I would be going to Stratford on Avon the next day. The next day I found her on the coach. She again ignored me and on this tour we were taken to an old fashioned inn where we were served a typical English lunch of roast beef in gravy, with potatoes. There were the bread, butter and dessert, of course. We were also served beer. Again I went for the bread and butter. This lady surfaced, calling me dearie and asked if she could share my lunch. She had everything from the beer to the beef to the dessert. And once again, when the meal was over we were strangers!

One evening my uncle and aunt took me to the theatre for Yul Brynner's 'The King and I'. If I had to die then, I would have been the most satisfied creature on earth. I am so grateful to my late uncle and aunt for making my trip so meaningful and adventurous while giving me all the homely comfort of chapathi, potato curry, rice and sambar. I realized on some of my foreign trips that it is possible to go someplace and just lie in a hotel room out of a sense of nervousness, fear, whatever, feeling miserable and lonely. That feeling of homely comfort, company and care I got on my first ever trip abroad made it the most memorable one ever in my life. It also gave me a tremendous sense of self confidence that stood me in good stead in all my subsequent foreign trips.

The high level of self-confidence that my family nurtured in me throughout, had been totally wiped out after my marriage - this got restored during my trip to London. From then on, nothing could stop me and I started moving on in life.

Complementing my self-confidence was my ability to interact with people freely and intelligently. At work there would always be overt and covert sexual advances by the male clientele, and this confidence enabled me to tactfully veer them off the track and still not lose their business. In the travel trade this was an occupational hazard as they called it in those days. One practice I stuck to throughout was not to get into personal relationships with clients or colleagues. My love affairs, which were exciting as long as they lasted, did not leave me with any bitterness when they ended. I worked with passion and enjoyed life to the hilt.

Sometime during the course of this period Amma asked that I go and stay with them and promised she would make sure that I was not made to feel I was living off them. I moved in and despite Appa's drinking sprees and crankiness, I really enjoyed being back with Amma. She would always try to cook something simple but special for me and never asked me any questions about the reasons for my marriage break up, nor did she ever remark on my outings with my boyfriend. That was truly amazing for a person coming from her background. I also never crossed the line and took care not to tread on my parents' space by inviting any of my friends home. I lived there but always met my friends outside. Looking back I can say that the bond of friendship Amma and I shared was invaluable.

The one significant aspect at this time was my entry into the third wave of the women's movement through the city based autonomous women's group Woman Power Group. My sister Asha was an active member and I had met some of the others when they came to her house. When she suggested that I attend one of the meetings with her I was terribly nervous to be in the company of women who were all excellent either in terms of academics or career or political commitment and experience. I had none of this and how would I fit? That was the beauty of the women's group. Nobody even attempted to make me uncomfortable by greeting me. It was just as if the waves were moving backwards in order to let the sand settle. If I smiled at one of them they smiled back at me and they continued talking, not excluding me but also not pressurizing me to talk.

There used to be reading sessions where each would take turns reading aloud. In between there would be some observation by one of us listening; the host of that meeting would quietly get up and make tea for all of us. Another member would help her in serving the tea. At the end of the meeting there was usually some high tea consisting of snacks and more tea. At this time, if any of the husbands or male friends of any of the members was waiting outside, they would be invited to join us. When we read Marilyn French's 'Women's Room,' I immediately connected with the experience of the protagonist. It was probably the first time I spoke out and said in a low voice to my neighbor that it sounded like my story.

There were also sessions when one of the members spoke about her life and experience. At many points of the narration we would have tears rolling down our cheeks. None of us asked why you cried, what you are feeling – it was a safe space where you could just give vent to your feelings without fear of being ridiculed or snapped at. It was here that I understood there was a sense and basis for my feeling of suffocation within my marriage and that walking out of it was a sensible step. What I thought was my unique problem was shared by almost all members of the group. We could see through our discussions that there is an expectation from women in our society to behave in a certain way and we women usually found it easier to melt and fall into the mold rather than question this expectation.

Almost all the members of the group were employed and the meetings would take place after 5 p.m. and sometimes on Sundays. Simultaneously, the group also addressed issues of custodial rape, living conditions of women and girls in social welfare and other hostels. We were all of maybe 12 members in the group; for any campaign it was only the 10 or 12 of us walking down the road. Those members who were in government service would be wary of publicly joining a campaign and a person like me in private service also had to be careful about not getting my photo into the newspapers.

I remember one instance when we took up the case of a girl staying in the local YWCA hostel; she complained that the rules were strict and the girls had to return to the hostel before 7 p.m.; this was problematic since sometimes their work stretched on beyond 6 pm. and commuting caused delays in returning to the hostel because of which the girls were locked out. We gave a representation that while a certain timing and discipline had to be maintained for the smooth running of any hostel, the punishment meted out was not right. The warden entered into an argument with us and accused the girl of 'loose morals.' We found this highly objectionable. We held a sit-in protest opposite the hostel and attracted quite a lot of attention.

I was not aware of it but my manager seems to have passed by and noticed me in the protesting group. The next day I was called into his cabin and the sales officer was also sitting opposite him. He looked at me and asked very sarcastically, 'You didn't tell us that you were a Communist!' I was perplexed. The sales officer then explained that I had been spotted in the protest meeting and that it is not allowed according to company rules. I apologised and promised that I would not go against the rule. Following this I was very careful.

During this phase of my life, there seemed to be more than 24 hours in a day. Work was a non-negotiable 8 – 9 hours, sometimes even more. I would go for my French class and then meet my boyfriend. After this, if there was a campaign I would go with our group members to help in whatever way I could. We took up quite a few campaigns like the enquiry into the custodial rape of Kamila Bi and later Shazia Bi, living conditions in working women's hostels, clinical trials of the injectable contraceptive by the government on innocent rural poor women; we also carried out short studies on the living conditions of girls in social welfare hostels, blind girls hostels, etc. We carried out protest rallies against rape and we would only be around 10 – 15 women walking the busy roads in the city. We would fling pamphlets into moving buses, hand them to passersby.

There were similar women's groups in Bombay, Delhi, Bangalore and Calcutta with whom we coordinated on national level campaigns. All the issues we took up as a campaign distressed me deep down. I felt the injustice in every nerve of my body. The range of issues reflected the range and intensity of atrocities being committed on women, starting from female feticide, to female infanticide, to child marriage to denial of education, to denial of nutrition to sexual abuse to rape to dowry harassment to domestic violence to discrimination at the workplace, to clinical trials of the banned contraceptive injectable on innocent, ignorant rural women and so the list is endless.

I was an also ran in our group, always hesitant to voice my view but all the time absorbing every single word, spoken or written and that has enriched my life beyond description. It is something I can never adequately measure. I learnt to analyze every written/unwritten word, spoken/unspoken thought and gestures, from a different viewpoint. There were so many things falling into place for me – my feelings, others' behavior, assumptions that became the norm for male/female behavior, so much of the smoldering despair and restlessness within me since the past seven years were getting explained through the Woman Power meetings! It was my birth as a feminist. It was rebirth for me, it was validating my refusal to adjust in the unequal relationship of my marriage.

Without any anger or malice, I started being myself at work and left it to those around me to adjust. This was becoming difficult for some people working with me, but by and large it was quite a cool scene. I remember that, once, a client, who was the head of a big research institute, had to go abroad and his secretary called up one day and asked to speak with the manager. I said the manager was not available and could I help. She reluctantly put me on to her boss. He said that he was to go to California for a conference and was exploring possibilities of getting the best deal in terms of visiting as many cities as possible within the direct route budget. In those days we had what was called a round the world ticket where you could travel to the east coast of America and return via the west coast or vice versa. It had minimum and maximum stay limits. I thought it would be suitable for him. He fixed up an appointment and visited our office and I recognized him as an old time neighbor. He did not know me but I just mentioned that we had been neighbors. We got down to business and then he said he would come the next day and look at the draft itinerary. The next day he came and asked me out for dinner. In the normal course, counter staff are not expected to entertain clients. But I was in a position where there was no manager and I was doubling up as sales and reservation counter staff and also managing the office. I could not refuse the invitation since it was a working dinner. I accepted and we met at the specified restaurant. He ordered a beer and I ordered a fresh lime soda. Over the starters, he asked if I was married and I quite frankly said I was but presently separated. He started playing with his glass of beer and sighed, saying how difficult it is to get the right partner in life. For example, he said, his head was burning with inventions and equations and when he went home his wife was complaining about a leaky tap or a wailing kid. I laughed and said, 'Just imagine that your wife is at home now with a guy whom she befriended, and is telling him that she is so fed up with a scientist husband who is all the time talking about his pet subject and not bothered whether her back is breaking due the heap of clothes she had to iron or she has a headache. How would you feel?' If he could, he would have hit me right there. But the fact that it was a public place prevented that and he simply got up and said that he was not hungry. I was fine with that so we went our separate ways. I thought I had messed up badly and we had lost the business. Thankfully, he did travel on our airline, but he left it to his secretary to carry out the formalities. I never heard from him again.

Sometimes I was not so lucky and we did lose the business, but I did not let on to even my colleagues as to what exactly transpired that we ended up losing the client. We gave excellent service and I felt that should suffice. In one case, I softly and frankly told the man that if he did not book on our airline, I would complain to his director that he had asked me to spend a weekend with him in Bangalore which I refused. That scared him so much that as long as he was posted in Hyderabad he never travelled on any other airline even if the route was inconvenient. I was getting good business and asked my boss why he was not making me manager since I was doing all the work anyway. He said that the position needed a man. I was not to be frazzled and asked what he expected a man to do that I could not do. He said that I could not organize and host a cocktails evening or take a travel officer of a company for drinks and lunch. There was one travel officer from a research institute whom all the airline offices and travel agencies tried to woo; he had a weakness for liquor and expected to be taken for lunch every Saturday where he would consume around a dozen bottles of beer and two plates of fried chicken. I took on the challenge put forth by my boss.

I threw a cocktails and dinner for travel agents and corporate clients and my wonderful boyfriend was there behind me to help out. The next issue was to tackle the travel officer and his beer lunches. I took him out once and it was trying to sit nursing a Fanta while he downed his several bottles of beer. When the gentleman was ready, I got a taxi to drop him off home. I thought about what to do since it was too trying for me to have a repeat Saturday. I then hit upon an idea that I simply have someone deliver him a dozen bottles of beer every Saturday morning and suggested the same to him. He, not surprisingly, agreed since it must have been a pain also for him to have me sit in front of him and watch him make a spectacle of himself. We got the business from his company regularly as long as I was working there.

I then asked my boss about my promotion. He promoted me as sales officer but still did not make me manager. My ex manager, who had also briefly tried out a job in Saudi, returned and another person in a travel agency was thinking of quitting his job. We three got along well and decided that we would pool all our knowledge, experience and influence to start a travel agency, with investment from a group of interested persons. It was an exciting venture and we started an agency called Sure Fix Tours & Travels. It was special for me because I had suggested the name and both the other guys were open to suggestions from me, treating me as one of them - on an equal footing. They saw me as a professional and that felt good.

It has always excited me to start a new venture right from interior décor to staff selection, setting up systems and practices. The guys left it all to me and got busy with getting business for the company. We really worked hard and reaped the benefits also. It so happened that my ex manager got a very good offer from the GSA[78] of a reputed airline company and left. The managing director was not systematic with the finances. This troubled me greatly. I was in a quandary because transparency has always been a highly cherished value for me. The carelessness of my boss was becoming uncomfortably distasteful to me.

---

[78]   GSA – General Sales Agency

Around this time there were constant efforts on my 85 year old Ammama's part to persuade me to return to my marriage. Her reasoning was that in a marriage there is only one man to deal with but when a woman is single the men get behind her like a pack of wolves.

I did not have such a good salaried job and faced with a financially insecure future I decided to give my marriage another chance in 1985. The other reason was that within Woman Power Group some frictions surfaced and a lot of changes took place. I was not the target at all and everybody was most sensitive and friendly with me but the tensions among them could not be hidden and it was unsettling for fragile people like me. The very force and strength which helped me to set my terms at the workplace seemed to lose strength and my insecurity returned. I probably could have spoken about my insecurities with someone from the group, but I lacked that level of self-confidence. I also tended to trivialize my insecurities, apprehensions and pain as much as I could. In this case I probably should have recognized my feelings to be as important as those of the other members. My feeling always was, 'Why bother others who are already coping with so much in their lives?' The feeling of being a burden on life itself may be a feeling many women have and it was a strong feeling in me. My sister Asha was there but she was going through a bad period dealing with the constant friction between Appa and her husband. She probably also had her own tensions in her family, besides which was the tension in the group. I decided to give my marriage another chance.

These mixed up feelings about what is right or wrong, do I want to be single or do I want to be married, what are my rights as wife, I recognized among a lot of women. Trading our bodies for a sense of security even if it meant jeopardizing our self-respect was a common phenomenon among women of my generation. Maybe I empathise so deeply with sex workers, because quite often I would feel that I was trading my body for security and creature comforts. I went to my marital home in Orissa and Arijit's brother Ranveer was very sick. He died that September shortly after I went. It was a shock for the whole family. Much against our wishes, Arijit and I had to carry out the last rites due to the fact that Ranveer's children were too young to do so. The elder brother, Shoor, came down from Gauhati and during his brief stay he talked to me privately and extracted a promise from me that I would not leave them again since, more than my husband I was a steadying influence on the family. I could not refuse. He went back to Gauhati and exactly two months later he died of a massive cardiac arrest. That shock was too much for Arijit who retreated into a shell as far as our relationship was concerned. Amma and Appa travelled all the way from Hyderabad to pay their condolences.

During the period of our separation Arijit had become an active member in the Trade Union and it was literally a case of his being married to it. This happens to anyone who takes up a leadership position in trade unions and I was glad for him because it weaned him off his other addictions. The city we lived in was just growing in the mid-1980s. A new office of a sales agency of Rathbone Airways opened and I got a job there. It was actually a cargo sales agency of airline. When I joined I introduced passenger sales and ticketing. We were three persons working there, one counter staff Aneek, one office assistant and myself. I needed to take a rickshaw every day and on the way back my colleague Aneek would drop me off on his scooter. I picked up the work fast and the airline's head office was very impressed with me. I was invited for a meeting to Calcutta. I took a night train and was met at the railway station by a seedy office assistant and put up in a really sleazy hotel. Later that morning I went to the airline office and forgot all about the discomfort of the hotel. The discussion with the team was invigorating and I was asked to attend a lunch hosted for travel agents that afternoon. It was at a swanky hotel the likes of which I had not visited earlier. The kind of people at the lunch was also different and I did feel a bit lost. One guy came forward and struck up a conversation with me. He was the manager of Rita Travels, Eastern Region and put forth an offer of employment as manager in their Bhubaneswar office since they were interested in expansion. I promised to revert once I returned.

On my return from Calcutta, Aneek and I visited the Rita Travels office in Bhubaneswar. It was in Hotel Sun Park's small shopping complex. We got the shutter opened and were suffocated by the stink of months old pigeon droppings in the fairly medium sized room. I decided to take up the job primarily because the hotel allowed the office to use the washroom of the hotel. I asked for appointing an office boy also and got the guy from my previous office. I told Aneek to wait for some more time before I got him in. Once I absorbed him, we started building up our clientele. I remember we both travelled all the way to Sambalpur and Rourkela in order to tap the industries. The companies found it strange to see a woman actually making sales visits. Even in the 1980s it was not a common feature for women to take up such jobs. There were women working as hotel housekeepers, receptionists, etc. in the hospitality sector, but the career of choice was usually that of teaching, other than government service. The local Indian Airlines booking office with whom we had an almost daily interaction, found my visits irksome. My colleague usually dealt with them but in his absence, I found it problematic.

At home, I lived my own life and was quite content. Munna, the Jeeves, was uncomfortable about my presence since he anticipated I would infringe on his territory and change his work pattern! I rarely went into the kitchen and this was probably not wise since he was not meticulous with regard to hygiene and basic healthcare – for example, he never boiled the milk thoroughly, and since we used to get fresh milk delivered on the doorstep it should have been boiled well. Given that my level of immunity was quite low from childhood, I ended contracting intestinal tuberculosis. The symptoms for this disease are very deceptive and my repeated attacks of lower abdominal pain and diarrhea were diagnosed as amebic dysentery. The doctor did not think of any further tests and I assumed his diagnosis was right. I just bore up with the pain and discomfort till the correct diagnosis and treatment commenced after my return to Hyderabad.

I had tried my best to appear confident and comfortable about giving my marriage another trial. My family however was not at all convinced. There used to be a constant watch kept not only through telephone calls but also through visits by one or other from the family on some pretext. Once my niece had a long holiday with us and towards the end, her husband joined her. This was followed by a visit from Asha and her husband. On their visits Arijit was quite cordial and took pains to entertain them. Somehow there was a false ring to this camaraderie that they detected and which I was actually blind to. Thinking back now, I see that I must have been happy to be employed and have comfortable living standards, with a married status, which kept at bay other men. I was not interested in physical intimacy or sexual relationships greatly and this was a relief for my husband. Since he had, during the period of our separation, got very involved in trade union activity, it kept him quite busy. I basically felt that I had a right to live off my husband since I had given a lot to my marriage. Anywhere else, I would have felt obligated, be it my parents or my siblings.

My experience in the first seven years of marriage rankled like nothing ever had and I was trying to get even in a manner of speaking. I was not clear as to who the enemy was – was it me, Arijit, his family or society? The helplessness and guilt I had felt earlier in my married life, I wanted to set right with my newfound feminism. There was no love in my heart, only the conviction that I had a right in that house. I was rather foolish, maybe, and overestimated my own strength both emotional and physical. I felt that I would live on my terms and nobody could stop me. It irritated me when Arijit kept calling me up every hour to just say 'I love you.' I knew it was his way of checking where I was and what I was doing, but it didn't faze me. I just played along and carried on with my work.

This surge of self-confidence I felt purely because of my involvement in the women's movement and in hindsight this decision could have been a hazardous one. Years later when I started conducting workshops to women in the development sector, my own experience was a relevant example of the need to exercise caution and common sense in our lives as women. I would repeatedly caution them not to exercise their new found confidence and knowledge carelessly and that the rebound of their euphoria could be hazardous.

Coming back to my personal life story, I remember that when we bought our first car, I had learnt driving and got my license in Hyderabad itself. When the second hand Fiat car arrived from Hyderabad, Arijit was still to have learnt to drive a four wheeler. The morning after we got it, I decided to go for a spin. I started the car and reversed and went bang into the gate post of our house. The car was badly dented but still strong. I coolly drove forward and out down the road. I drove to a mechanic and got him to bang the dents out as much as possible. When I returned, Arijit, my brother Kavi and the driver who had driven it from Hyderabad were all standing out, waiting for me. I drove in, parked and got out. I said that I had got some of the dent beaten out and the mechanic across the road said that there was no other damage to the car. The purpose of my going out even after the crash was to keep my self-confidence intact and I decided that come what may I would be cool. Kavi was literally holding his sides to stop himself laughing and Arijit of course was simply stunned at what I had done. Above all he could not believe that I had the gall to be so cool about it. Only the driver smiled and said, 'You did the right thing, Amma, by going on driving. If you had not you would never got over the fear.' Reversing has always been a problem with me. Maybe reversal per se is an issue in my life!

From then on I made it a point to drive across to the post office and also went on long drives to Khandagiri, a Buddhist shrine. I always did this early in the morning since Arijit would not have woken up. The relationship was making me rough and irritated. It was not long before things blew up between us and matters reached an impasse very soon. It was frightening for me because in one of our quarrels Arijit's temper just flew of the handle.

Shaking all over, I asked him to leave the room immediately and as soon as he left, I bolted the door from inside. Trembling with shocked anger I lay down and curled up on the floor. When I heard him going out, I quickly went and fetched myself enough water to last me the night. He tried to get me to open the door on his return but I refused. He was in the guest room and the next morning he knocked and said he wanted to hand me a letter. I opened the door just enough and took the letter. He had written that he and I had irreconcilable differences and could not live under one roof and since the house was rented out to him in his capacity as an officer in National Bank of India, I, Usha would have to move out within a month's time.[79] The gall of the letter angered me. He thought I would be afraid, upset or display my anger. I did nothing – just tucked the note into my handbag, got ready and quickly went off to my office.

Later, I visited an elderly lady friend, showed her the letter, explained what had happened and asked if there was any women's hostel I could move into. She was in an awkward situation because she liked me very much but Bhubaneswar was not so developed that she could offer me shelter. She was afraid of inviting censure from her husband for interfering in other people's personal matters and also that Arijit was well known for his illustrious family background; I was the outsider, so she would invite criticism from friends and relatives for supporting me. It was inconceivable in that time and age in a state like Orissa, that a woman would walk out on her marriage so brazenly. She said that the best thing would be for me to inform my family and that it would be unsafe for me to shift into a hostel because Arijit would have friends who would collude with him and make out that I was mentally unstable. I gave her my sister's telephone number and got back to the room which was my home for almost a week.

I did not eat anything. I would go off to work because I knew that Arijit would not come and publicly force me to do anything. I would get home early from work and send the cook off on an errand so as to pack my stuff. I decided that I would not leave behind anything that I had brought into that house. It was conveyed to me that Asha my sister was coming and I asked Aneek to take her directly to the office. I had packed everything and lined them up. Aneek brought a taxi and we quickly pushed everything including the gas cylinder and stove into the taxi. Asha asked Aneek to dump all the stuff in the

---

[79]   I still have this note with me

hotel where he had booked a room for us and she took me to a restaurant for lunch. I could not talk. She coaxed me to eat since I needed energy to travel. We were booked to leave two days later.

I was thoroughly shaken and trembling with fear at the immensity of what I had done, the likely consequences and whether Asha and I could handle the situation if Arijit traced us to the hotel. We were quite sure he would and he did. It was easy, because Munna, the cook had seen us loading stuff into the taxi, and it was not difficult tracing the taxi. It took him only a half day and he landed up the next afternoon with his friend. Though the room was booked in Asha's name the manager of the hotel had seen me and knew I was Arijit's wife. When Arijit was refused entry into the room, the friend asked if he could come in and talk. She let him in and when he saw me lying all curled up and trembling, he said he would persuade Arijit to leave me alone but that he was unlikely to succeed.

That evening they went away but as anticipated, Arijit did land up the next afternoon, with the Jeeves in tow carrying a tiffin box. We realized there was no way we could avoid him and so let him in. When he wanted to speak with me alone my sister refused. We realized then that even if we cried for help, we would not stand a chance since we were on his territory and friends and strangers alike were his allies. He asked the cook to apologise for being the cause of the whole quarrel. That poor boy fell to the floor weeping and asked me to beat him but to return home. He then handed the tiffin box containing fried fish! Arijit tried to push Asha out from between us and persuade me to return home. I just kept saying, I'm going to my home. He sat for almost two hours and then left saying I would regret this decision. Once he left, Asha opened the tiffin box of hot fried fish and after tasting some to make sure it was not poisoned, she started feeding me small bits of it!

The next day my colleague Aneek accompanied us to the railway station and when we reached, we found my elder sister-in-law walking on the platform looking for us. She spotted us and tried to speak with me. I remember her pushing Asha aside saying she wanted to speak with me only. Once the train started pulling out of the platform we heaved a sigh of relief and as we moved further from the town, I started feeling better. I was clear that I must get a divorce as soon as possible.

My return did not evoke any taunts or sarcasm from family or friends. It was taken as just one more experience and I moved on from there. The management had changed hands in Sure Fix Travels but the post of manager was open. The same group of staff and director who had gifted me an electric mixer on my leaving for my marital home now welcomed me as if I had never left at all. There were no questions or curiosity. The level of comfort and understanding was truly wonderful and unforgettable. I was looking for a change and seeing an opening in Step Up Travels for the post of sales manager, I moved there.

It was at this time that my physician felt I needed to undergo further tests for my frequent attacks of dysentery. There were consultations with other doctors as well and it was decided that I should start off on a course of the anti-tuberculosis drugs, since the diagnosis was that I was affected by T.B. of the intestine. This illness came at a time when I was simultaneously dealing with a new, performance oriented job and getting together evidence to file for my divorce; the fragility I felt at this point of time was probably one of the worst I have ever felt. The steroid medication increased my body weight and gave me an elephantine feeling. Rajamama was too hurt by what had happened to me to personally handle my divorce petition; the lawyer who took it up was somehow also feeling delicate to ask me for details of what went on and he was counseling me to give the marriage another trial. I got sick of it and sat down and wrote the petition myself. He then put it in legal language and I only requested that when the case came up for hearing he ensure that it was in camera and not public.

Arijit of course did not take any of the summonses and it was finally advertised in the local newspapers before the hearing. I had to go to Kalingapatnam since that was where we had got married. I had no idea if Arijit would come for the hearing. My younger brother Srikar and his wife accompanied me. As my legal counsel predicted, Arijit did not turn up and the judgment was passed ex parte. I was awarded the divorce with the clause that I be paid a monthly maintenance of Rs.500 by Arijit. That was the end of the second phase of my married life. I never got the maintenance and decided to move on rather than get into legal hassles.

I was getting more and more involved in the women's movement and it was the time when Woman Power split into two – one focusing on research and the other retaining the activist role. So were born Aastha, the Research Centre on the one side and Saathin, the activist group, on the other. In between there was the formation of the Katnam Vyatirekata Committee which comprised of women like Amma and other women of her age group as well as members from Woman Power, to investigate the phenomenal rise in dowry murders, where young women were set on fire for not being able to meet the ever rising dowry demand from their husband's family.

I made a few visits to the burns wards in the government hospital to see these women who suffered from severe burn injuries and even now I get images of women burnt beyond recognition giving their dying declaration that they alone were responsible for the extreme step they took. The disappointment and frustration we felt in such instances cannot be described but the logic was that one cannot expect any other response from these women who knew they were dying and did not want to jeopardize the safety their surviving siblings and parents. The KVC[80] prevailed upon the police not to take such declarations as sufficient evidence to absolve the husband and his family from the crime. This committee had a good impact on the police machinery and worked effectively in helping bring about the legislation in the Prevention of Dowry Act.

I was careful about not getting openly involved, in view of my job. It was probably this caution on my part that gave many of the other members a feeling that I did not whole heartedly participate in the group's activities. There is nothing that can measure the relevance and meaning the involvement in the group gave me and through me touched the lives of thousands of women in different corners of India.

While working in Step Up Travels I got to undertake my second foreign trip and this time it was to Hong Kong, courtesy Indi American Airlines. It was not a trip I enjoyed and the only enjoyable part was when I was able to succeed in getting a set of baking equipment for my sister-in-law, Latha, who had a passion for baking. I was communicating through gestures with a Chinese speaking salesgirl in the local supermarket because all of them only understood Chinese.

On my return I started planning to branch out as a freelance travel agent where I could use the office infrastructure of a travel agency for finalizing travel bookings of my clients, give the booking to the agent and in turn getting the 9 % commission as well as any incentive the airline gave the agent,

---

[80]　KVC –Katnam Vyatirekata Committee – committee against dowry

which could be anything like 15%. My work in the travel field from 1980 to 1985, had earned me the reputation of a thorough professional who always gave the best services. I was therefore assured of a sizeable clientele who would not expect anything more than good service from me. I advertised in the newspapers giving the telephone numbers of Appa and Rajamama since both the houses were in the same compound and when the response to the ad started coming in, I was literally running up and down the stairs of both the houses. I came to an agreement with one travel agent and it was tough but enjoyable work. My health was improving and I helped the research centre Aastha with translations from Hindi for some research work. I was filled with pride when I learnt that one of my translated poems was selected as part of the research publication.

It was 1989 and my sister Asha took up an assignment to conduct a 10 day national workshop for women working in NGOs[81] and the participants were to be women from all over the country. She asked if I would like to form part of the facilitating team and said that I would be paid an honorarium for the same. The organisers invited me for the meeting at Together We March a funding organization based in Hyderabad, along with Asha. I went, not because I was any great development expert, but because I was fairly fluent in many languages. Actually, it was Asha's weight that I rode on. I don't know what I would have done without her staunch support at the most critical of times. This was a turning point in my life and I can now say that I finally found my calling and mission in this lifetime. Asha gave me a set of literature to read up which I did religiously. I sat and wrote down the

---

[81]   NGO – nongovernmental organisations

plans she drew up and typed it out later. I also typed out the letters of invitation to the various feminists inviting them to participate as resource persons for specific sessions in the workshop. I left the planning to her but accompanied her to the meetings at the TWM[82] office. Leela (who worked as architect in a government office and member of Woman Power) also formed part of the team. The workshop was to take place in Bangalore and Shubha Kumar working with a development organisation in Bangalore, helped with the local coordination. I did all the secretarial work to start with. Later, when the actual workshop started, I took on a whole lot more work like logistics, translation, daily documentation of each session, and daily accounting. While I knew I had to do all this work, nothing had prepared me for a quite different role that awaited me on the eve of the workshop.

When we reached Indian Centre where the workshop was to take place, and settled down, I decided to take a walk around. I spotted six women sitting on the steps of a room, all looking ill at ease and lost. I went over and introduced myself. Three women were from Bihar and three from Orissa. It was clear that with the exception of two, the other women were uncomfortable conversing in English. I switched to Hindi and the Bihar women felt relieved. But the women from Orissa were still uncomfortable since they were not fluent in Hindi either. I don't know how it happened, because I had never uttered a word of Oriya as long as I lived in Orissa, though I kept listening and absorbing the language in order not miss anything that was being said; I started forming words and sentences to myself and then repeating them to the women. The excitement and pleasure of the women at hearing me speak in Oriya are indescribable. I then started practicing

---

[82] TWM – Together We March

conversations, translating session content within my mind, so that I could ensure that the women from Orissa felt included. This transformation in me is still unfathomable.

What is the pull I felt towards these women? I realized that it was very simply a strong feeling that nobody should feel excluded from a conversation. I took on the role of hostess in the sense that I kept a look out for any sign of discomfort, feeling of neglect, illness, dislike for some particular type of food, and informed Asha about it. I remember Asha's amusement when I mentioned that maybe there should be plain 'dal' in addition to the sambar so the women from Bihar and Orissa could enjoy their food. She thought I was being fussy as I used to be with Arijit's tastes. But she realized my point and instructed the kitchen to serve a dish of non-spicy 'dal' also at every meal. This helped us prevent a possible confrontation about the food arrangements. The institute served beef and I noticed that the women from Andhra, Orissa and Bihar were upset about it. I alerted Asha and she asked the mess not to serve beef or pork. Everyone was happy with the plain dal and once a week chicken curry. This workshop made me realise the importance food and language play in helping establish comfort zones for people when they are in alien territory. This is a point I keep in mind when I travel to any foreign country and I always carry some Indian food and one of my favourite Indian music discs.

One of the Bihar women, Sunanda, had obviously travelled with what was suspected as Kala Azar[83]. It was difficult since she was suffering from high fever and the doctor said she must be isolated from the rest but no hospital would admit her. He prescribed some medication to bring down the fever but there was no medication for the disease since it was something

---

[83]   Kala Azar – a viral fever caused by the bite of sand fly which is prevalent in Bihar and some parts of north India

restricted to Bihar and neighbouring regions. I had not even heard about such a disease. I must say Sunanda had some grit. She would insist on attending the sessions and we had to arrange a space for her away from the rest of the women but so she could hear the Hindi translations. Asha had warned me not to get carried away by emotion and think I was superwoman. She said that she and Leela would attend to Sunanda! There was one woman, Radha from Tamilnadu with a month old daughter. She was accompanied by her husband who asked if he could attend the workshop on her behalf. We strictly refused and said that he could babysit, so Radha attended the sessions. We offered to babysit also if he wished to leave. It was probably the first time he was changing nappies and putting an infant to sleep!

To me every woman at the workshop was a mirror image of me, reflecting the same stormy mind filled with 'irrational, mad thoughts,' a body wanting to stretch and bend to touch the earth deep below the ground, arms wanting to reach upwards and hold a handful of the blue white clouds in the sky. In that workshop every woman, when talking about herself revealed quite unconsciously, how much she wanted to *be,* but was behaving as she was expected to. It angered me that we as women were not allowed to *be.* What this workshop did for me and the 50 odd women present, cannot be adequately described in words.

From here on my story would seem very woman centric. My life became so. My interaction with men on the home front was minimal, restricted only for practical needs; my social life had ceased. There was probably a reason for this. The passing remark my boyfriend Pratik had made, about his youth causing an erosion in our relationship just because I was 10 years older than him, determined me that I would never

ever get into a relationship with a person where my age or other physical, psychological attributes would seem to make me vulnerable. Except for continuing my friendship with Parimala (as long as she was alive) and Rama (my childhood friend of 66 years) there was nothing else. They were comfortable to be with. They always joked that if they wanted to visit me they would have to go to some remote village since my house was always locked. In the office the interaction with my male colleagues was again restricted to what was necessary. My life truly revolved around the 50 women, their work, and their lives for almost a decade. It was an obsession and that is why I see it as a calling.

The elation we all felt at the workshop in the summer of 1989 cannot be adequately described. The getting together, sudden freedom not only from their routine organizational work but also from their homes and their families was mind-blowing for the fifty women. These were women who had come to a totally strange training workshop, tentative, nervous, expecting to pick up a few craft skills that they could in turn go back and teach the women in their work area. They had drawn rigid lines between teacher and taught and expected either instructions or lectures; instead, to their growing amazement they were discovering that the theory and knowledge they had vaguely heard about, was not something that was cut off from their everyday lives but was rooted in their daily experience. This was a relief and an unexpected reward for them. They realized that all the theory drew on the insights and techniques they had evolved in the course of their own work. It made no sense to them initially that the workshop was actually a process of creating the space for themselves to reflect and theorize on their own activity. They could not believe that they could discuss even their most irrational feelings or tentative hopes without apprehensions of being ridiculed or trivialized. It is difficult to describe the responses as well as the sense of release and energy that was generated in that workshop. The hope, excitement and joy of being part of the process many of the women recollected for several years. The fact that the women came from totally different linguistic states, speaking Telugu, Tamil, Hindi and Oriya added a unique flavor to the whole process. Confronted by the women's determination to make the most of their time together, strengthen themselves and deepen their understanding of their work, we as the training team felt invigorated to ensure that the best possible process would emerge. The workshop turned out to be a remarkable process.

We had planned the workshop with care, dwelling on the content, its appropriateness and relevance to the potential trainees. We had chosen the resource persons with deliberation. These resource persons were women whose theory was solidly supported by practical experience as activists. And yet when they came face to face with the trainees, and perceived their hunger for knowledge and their need for conceptual tools, the resource persons adapted themselves to the need; straight forward lecture presentations got transformed by a process in which elaborate and complex concepts were broken down. The trainees grasped it all with total ease.

What happened that week in May was significant for all of us. The line dividing the trainers, and trainees was wiped out as the trainers and the trainees were absorbed in the process of learning from each other. The problem we saw for the future was, creating a system or mechanism to support and nurture what had begun during that workshop. Many hopes and needs were roused during the week – the problem we saw staring us in the face was how to protect those hopes from being trampled in the bustle and cynicism of a practical routine which in the interests of efficiency allows no space for articulating women's problems?

While we as the facilitating team had been ruminating about this, the participants were also having discussions in their own regional and cross regional discussions. On the concluding day of the workshop when Mr. Murthi, Director of TWM came to address the gathering, Rupavathi, from Tamilnadu became the spokesperson for the entire group and said that if the process that had started, and the thinking that had been set in motion had to be sustained and grown, TWM needed to support it and this could only be done by having a woman within its structure to look into matters concerning women's training; she said that they felt I would suit the job perfectly.

Asha had cautioned me that I may be asked by Murthi to take forward the work but this kind of statement by the women at the workshop left me with no bargaining power in terms of salary, position, etc. Murthi could see my predicament and said that I could consider working part time for six months and decide what I wanted to do. For me it was the turning point in my life.

I saw what my calling was, in one sense. I was constantly connecting the theoretical discussions of the resource persons with the practical experience as narrated by one of the 50 women each day. For me, seeing the manifestation of an issue in the context of caste, religion, family, or violence in the life of one of the women present at the workshop was an affirmation of the need for the women's movement to spread and permeate – widely and deeply. This sufficed to help me make up my mind. I could feel the shift within – from *ME* to *US*. The *US* was so vast, so spread out, so diverse, and so meaningful. My life, my tensions, contradictions, seemed to fade back in this huge canvas that was unfolding both within and outside the workshop hall daily.

I doubt if anyone in TWM even thought about the giant stride it had taken in the context of women's equality in the development sector. The workshop was a trailblazer and the effect of that initiative changed the commonly understood concept of development and set in motion a shift in the male-female power dynamics. It brought onto centre stage women working in the NGO sector, it provided them an understanding however limited it may be, of women and empowerment, it gave them a voice and a fire to question inequality. This kind of change took place in other parts of the world only a few years later. I cannot fathom why such a historic shift was not highlighted adequately. I would think it was because of a north-south divide. Even to this day this distinction continues. Given the fact that two of the states were in the south may be one reason.

As project coordinator in TWM I had to do the compilation of the national workshop report, help Asha with the editing, shop for reasonably priced but good printers, design the cover, make a list for distribution etc. I had managed to take down copious notes, and supplemented them with audio taping. Transcribing audio tapes was no easy job. It literally meant reliving the whole workshop for me. Anita helped by taking down notes which I dictated and then typing the same on the typewriter. A friend recommended I try to get a printer's reference from Ramesh of Sriya Xerox in Hyderabad. I went to him with all the typed sheets and he said that I should keep a Xerox copy with me and he would do the printing work for us. It meant that he typed the whole manuscript onto the computer as first draft. Once the correction was done, we finalized the size and font. I then had to go to another layout artist for the cover design. This work went on till 8.30 – 9 p.m. every day, usually since the company did not want to lose its Xerox clientele. Since Anita was too young and inexperienced to handle the work and there was nobody else who knew much about printing, I was wholly responsible. The end product, in the form of a report…' evoked an exhilaration that wiped out all the exhaustion.

At the same time as I was getting ready the report, I had to plan visits to the various states, fix dates for the regional workshops, do the necessary correspondence and get to know my office colleagues. Between June 1989 and June 1996 I must have covered the length and breadth of India. I visited places I had only seen as dots on the physical map of India. It was good that it was possible for Leela, member of Woman Power and co facilitator of the national workshop at Bangalore to accompany me in the first six months of field visits and regional workshops. We made Tamilnadu our first region.

Our first stop was in Mayiladuthurai to visit the NGO doing women's development work. It was a partner supported by TWM and two women workers, Shamala and Ruth had attended the national workshop. We had taken a bus from Madras and while we were a bit surprised that there was nobody to receive us on arrival, we did not find anybody even when we went over to their office. It was a small town and when we mentioned Shamala's name to a few people near the office, they quickly called her and she came running expressing surprise over our visit. I said that we had intimated her organization head and showed her the copy of the letter and telegram. Seeing our need to refresh ourselves she found us a hotel with miserable facilities and waited while we freshened up. The dingy walls of the room, and leering looks of the men hanging around outside only strengthened my resolve to work towards a change. When we reached the office, a resentful set of staff were present but the 'boss' was not to be seen. I got to see the 'development activists' in the NGO. The men with unkempt hair, straggly beards, dressed in collarless zebra striped T shirts and veshti, with a thin towel thrown over the shoulder or tied round the head.

Coming to think of it, the dress was in a way, formal Tamilian! It was not possible for us to start off a discussion according to our agenda without the boss. I took a quick decision to carry out a regular inspection and stated that I would like to check the staff attendance records, minutes register and the accounts books. Within 10 minutes of my making known my decision, the boss landed up. He demanded to know why I was asking for the registers and files. I showed him the carbon copy of the letter written to him by our Director stating that I represented TWM and should be extended all cooperation during my visit to the organization. The statement was so broad that it could cover anything under the sun. It had the desired effect, in that the NGO head immediately arranged two village visits for us to enable us to meet the community women and his attitude to Shamala was as if she was the head of the organization. While Shamala's rapport and credibility with the community women was clearly visible, what surfaced was the total disconnect between what was described as happening on the ground and the reality as related by the community women.

I felt there was a pattern to all projects focusing on women's development whichever part of the country I visited. Initially the promise by the NGO was to deliver in the form of easy interest and repayment schedule, loans to the CBWGs. The NGO head also visited them and spoke at the meetings. Once the groups were formed and the women started savings, only

Shamala would make brief visits once in two weeks to collect the savings. There was never any visit by the NGO head. One year was completed when I visited and they had not got any loan nor did they get their money back. Even Shamala's visits we were told had of late, totally stopped. We returned to the office to find it locked. At the staff meeting the next day, the 'boss' whom everyone called 'Anna[84],' was very solicitous and left it to Shamala to manage us. He did not know how to deal with Leela and me. Shamala was a vibrant, bold young woman with a good singing voice and a hard worker. She smilingly muttered to us that the 'boss' did not know how to please us since we were not great eaters, or drinkers or 'manizers[85]!' I told her that I would put down what we saw and heard, in my report. She smiled helplessly.

Shamala came to the hotel the next morning and accompanied us to the bus stand from where we proceeded to Kumbakonam. Here Kanakavalli had just started a NGO (DOW) [86]and she did not seem to be sure of what she wanted to do. There was a lot of poverty, and the women were affected acutely by this poverty, but Kanakavalli can only be described as a staid Iyengar very conscious of her caste. When we asked her why she decided to get into this kind of developmental work she said that she had been advised by Mr. Mukunda Iyer of Mahatma Gandhi Ashram. I found that followers of Gandhian thought believed that women and girls who were disturbed or restless could reign in this restlessness by getting involved in community work. This observation was something that disturbed and irritated me at that point of time. Later reflections left me with a sense that it was a deliberate attempt

---

[84]   Anna – Elder brother
[85]   Manizers – antonym of womanizer
[86]   DOW – Development of the Women

173

to keep women in the background on the grounds that women were the 'weaker sex.'

Anyway, here was Kanakavalli of DOW with about 200 women whom she mobilized with what promises she only knows, and not a clue as to how to move further and do something meaningful. Leela felt that there was some possibility of changing Kanakavalli's thinking and that she could help the women she had mobilized to strategically move ahead. I did not have any such hope, but agreed to recommend support from TWM for her. Lakshmiammal was working under the umbrella of DOW but in a different set of villages. She was a single mother of two growing kids. She suffered a lot in her marriage and it was not easy for her to live alone with her children in a small town in Tamilnadu. Someone entered her life with concern and compassion and they entered into a relationship, which was, in a way, a safeguard for Lakshmiammal. He had quite a different agenda. He wanted Lakshmiammal to float her own NGO and he would manage it.

With the UN Declaration of the Decade for Women in the Nairobi Women's Conference in 1985, there was a lot of research done on women's status, and situations in what was called developing or third world countries, resulting in efforts on the part of the first world countries to support women's development in third world countries. A lot of money was available and very few women's organisations. Almost all over India men took advantage of this opportunity and used women they sometimes did not even know, to head organisations they set up and their sole motive was to access funds. Quite often it would be men who were not remotely connected to the voluntary development work at all.

The autonomous women's groups in India had taken a stand not to accept foreign funding. This funding was finding its way to NGOs, and from what I was seeing, a lot of it was coming into Tamilnadu. NGOs which were floated by seasoned development workers, by total newcomers and which used women's names and faces to access the funds were the recipients of the funds. The seasoned development NGO heads used some of the feminist language and there was no dearth of poor women or villages or slums or issues affecting women to be shown as the beneficiaries of various initiatives. In the early 1990s I remember that Funds for Women, USA had invited me to be on its advisory council so that it could refer some of the India based grant applications from India to me. I took the role with all earnestness and it was quite shocking that all the applications were from NGOs headed by men and many of the addresses given in the applications were fraudulent. I could see then that the international focus must have been the pressure on TWM also to focus on women's development and therefore the shift in focus from community to community women took place even in TWM'S funding criteria.

Insofar as the three women, Shamala, Kanakavalli and Lakshmiammal were concerned, Leela and I thought that if we involved them in regular training programs, they would be able to handle the NGOs they worked in quite effectively. What we did not think about was that there was a political consciousness that we in autonomous women's groups had, which these women lacked and that cannot come about just by their feeling oppression or inequality or through training. Added to this were the kind of environment they lived in, the inaccessibility to feminist groups and the limitation of our own support to them. It is a very difficult struggle to persevere and survive with feminist beliefs and practices anywhere in India even now and in the late 1980s to expect women to do so in small towns like Mayavaram and Kumbakonam was asking for the moon. The fact that they tried is in itself a significant step forward for them.

As Leela and I proceeded further into our Tamilnadu field visits in an attempt to assess the level of understanding NGOs had about women's development we grew more and more despondent. It was quite amazing that even the most basic of conveniences were not thought about for women in NGOs in the late 1980s. A separate toilet with running or stored water for women, for example, which is considered basic, was totally lacking in all the NGOs we visited. Even in NGOs with a minimum of 10 women working in the office there was no toilet. These were NGOs that claimed to address issues like female infanticide, exploitation, vocational training etc. There was also a rather amusing belief among NGOs that people working there must do their own work, but there was a hierarchy to this. The women working at the community level or community animators were the lowest rung. They had the responsibility of catering to all the creature comforts of the higher up persons and their visitors. I always found that the boss (in those days, male), would have a separate toilet and that would be the only clean one in any NGO office.

Despite all these drawbacks my journey into the development field was eye opening and full of richness. In 1979 Woman Power validated my yearning for respect, and recognition as a human being. And this national workshop ten years later, brought 60 reflections of me, which I was later to discover, had a thousand more reflections across the country. I was transformed – my defined family space, my search for love, companionship, sex, was irrelevant. What I was searching for (quite unconsciously) I had found. I knew that all my intelligence, negotiating skills, energy, caring and affection lay with these 50 women and the 100s more they represented. The turning point in my life crystallized. In June 1989 I joined as part time coordinator but I ended up doing a 24 x 7 job, for Rs.2, 000 per month.

Even in 1989 a monthly income of Rs.2,000 was hardly adequate. Thankfully my sister Asha took on the role of benefactor for almost 15 years. She would discreetly stock up my kitchen with groceries. Every few months she would call me to her home and throw a pile of saris and ask me to select a few since she was tired of wearing them. She had hardly worn any of them and actually wanted me to have a good wardrobe. In order that I did not ever feel left out she would insist that I have dinner every evening. Even to this day it makes me cry that she would always make time to come into the kitchen and rustle up some dish in addition to what was on the dinner table. She would then stand around, picking bites for herself from my plate and chat as I ate. She never did this for her own children but she always did this for me.

I thus had the sense of being independent but was totally cared for by this wonderful sister of mine. I don't think anyone else has been so fortunate. But good things don't always last and one summer when we all went to Kashmir for a holiday, Asha and her husband were killed in a landslide. I don't know how I bore the shock. It is unreal even 15 years later that such a disaster took place. I kept thinking for many years that Asha was somewhere, keeping a watch on me. But time has blunted my optimism.

I was allowed to continue in my job more out of compassion than anything else. I learnt to manage within my means. I kept working and someone or other was always kind enough to drop by and leave a bag of rice, sometimes sugar, sometimes other groceries. I lived a careful and frugal life. On a slowly increasing salary year on year I managed to make both ends to meet.

But how long could I continue to work? I grew older and was not able to travel extensively. Six months before my 58th birthday I was told that I would have to retire on my birthday. And so my only source of income dried up. I was kindly given a sum of Rs.50,000 in recognition of my steadfast services. Being a non profit organization TWM had no provision for pension.

As time went on and my money started dwindling I started selling my few gold ornaments in order to survive with dignity. When I knew it was no longer possible to continue living independently I took the suggestion of a neighbor and came here...

A Matter of Urgency

"Ma, send me some fresh tea...this tea tastes awful...how can I wake up with such ditchwater...?

Basanti heard her son ranting on...with a sigh she put aside the 'saag' she was chopping, heaved her worn and heavy body off the floor. She washed her hands and wiping them against her sari, pulled her 'pallav' forward to cover her head. Carefully removing the sooty pressure cooker of half cooked rice and 'dal' off the flickering kerosene stove, she placed a saucepan on it and measured out two cups of milk and water into it. Her lips puckered and almost immediately tightened into a thin line of determination...determination not to allow even the hint of impatience enter her jagged mind. True ... this was the third cup of tea he was having replaced... but then, poor boy, he worked so hard and slept late most nights... almost immediately she heard the echoes of her 'bahu's' voice, soft and gentle... "But Ma, I work too, I leave home at nine every morning and close office at 6 every evening...after that I go to the 'haat' at least three times a week...besides rushing to the fish market at five in the morning at least three days a week so that the fridge is well stocked with the variety of fish that is palatable to your son's sensitive taste buds. I take care to wake him up every morning with gentle words and a soft touch so he won't feel the harshness of a new day breaking in on him, unbeckoned...I don't find it difficult to wake up on my own and fix my own coffee...so why does he find it so hard?"

Basanti had then fondly caressed her 'bahu's' head and said, "Suchi...my favourite 'bahu' Suchi, you are special, you do everything so well, you are so talented... so quick and efficient... but why do you ask such strange questions... why do you tease your mind with complicated thoughts? Go now and wash ...comb your hair... change your sari... Bholu will be coming any minute now and it wouldn't do for you to be looking so unkempt, like the 'chakirani' who cleans our house."

She recalled Suchi walking away taut and unrelenting. Pulling her gaze back from the past, she saw the milk was simmering. She added tea leaves and sugar, stirring all the time. She lifted the saucepan from the stove, covering it and settling it on the platform. She placed the pressure cooker back on the stove and remembered that Bholu would also expect his customary 'paans.' She peered into the refrigerator and not finding the pack of readymade paans in its cellophane cover, she realized that the tiresome errand boy Rama had once again forgotten her instruction to roll out a set of six 'paans' in the morning. She would now have to scurry around doing this job also when all she wanted was to stretch her legs and back for a while. Wearily hobbling back to the kitchen, she felt someone standing behind her. Looking back she found Bholu's father standing hesitantly at the door... he nervously cleared his throat, twisting his neck to the right and then the left shoulder; "Aaannnnhhh.... I seem to be catching a cold or something... mmm... listen ..., do you think I could have just a half cup of tea... just half cup... not more... too much tea upsets the stomach, naa...?" he pleaded.

Basanti looked at him expressionlessly and after a significant pause, said, "Hanh... but remember, you won't get your usual cup after breakfast... I can't spend all the household money on tea for you at all odd times..."

"Yes… yes… of course … hari Om…hari Om…" the old man muttered and walked away, rubbing his arms. Basanti cast him a baleful look grumbling 'Catch cold indeed, he just needs some excuse…" She balanced the tea cup and cellophane wrapped 'paan' in her right hand and walked towards Bholu's bedroom. At the entrance she paused and called to her daughter in law, "will you take this tea to Bholu, bahu…" Pushing aside the curtain Suchi took the teacup from Basanti's hand without so much as giving her a glance. "Bholu, jaan…, here is your tea… and get yourself out of bed fast because it is getting late for me … if I have to drop you off at work … I need the car today … important client meeting… shake it man…!" Hearing Suchi's loud and sarcastic voice Basanti winced for her dear Bholu… he was such a gentle soul. Just then she spotted Rama and waddled off towards him to inspect the small fish he was cleaning … Bholu's favourite dish was small fish lightly smeared with a touch of mustard paste, and crisp fried in mustard oil. She gave Rama a gentle push and asked him to clean the fish fast. In the kitchen she seasoned the 'dal' and then set the frying pan sizzling with mustard oil to fry the fish.

As Rama settled down to clean the fish Basanti's husband saw him and said, 'Arrey, Rama, you've come… give me my breakfast… I have to go to the 'Mutt' for the spiritual discourse… fast… I am late already…"

Basanti glared balefully at her husband and walking up to him, hissed, "Can't you wait a bit…?" How many things will we manage at the same time…? Bholu's food has to be ready … he will be needing hot water for his shave … as it is, bahu is in a hurry to leave early today… Hey Bhagawan, and in all this rush you also want to rush to your ashram… I feel like running away somewhere … and all because of you … why can't you go and live in the village … you won't give me one moment's peace…"

Just then Suchi emerged from the bedroom dressed in a crisp blue silk sari, with matching ear tops, ring and a quaint bracelet on her delicate wrist. Her eyes fell on the heap of fish lying near the backdoor and she wrinkled her nose against the smell. Rama was carefully rubbing each fish between thumb and forefinger to remove the scales. Bholu happened to walk out from the bedroom to fetch himself a glass of water. "Do you have to eat freshly bought, freshly fried fish on a Wednesday morning" Suchi asked, poking him gently in the rib.

Bholu shrugged indifferently and replied, "I don't, but Ma seems to think it necessary so that's it."

Not one to give up so easily Suchi persisted, "why does everything Ma want done in this house centre around you only... she grudges the occasional extra cup of tea that Baba wants ... the poor old man squirms like a worm before he can muster up the courage to ask for it ... she resents his very presence in the house ... he has as much right to stay with us she does, naa ...as for me, I don't know what she wants from me ... as long as I was doing all the work she resented that I was managing the house and felt slighted... on your suggestion I left it to her and ... most days I skip breakfast, and lunch out because she is so preoccupied with your work... her complaint is that I don't take care of my husband ... what care is she taking of her husband...?"

Hearing this Basanti felt like every word was a whiplash on her poor Bholu's back... why was Bholu keeping quiet, she wondered... why did he not ask the shameless hussy to shut up ...what kind of modern thinker was she ... no sindoor on her forehead, no glass bangles on her wrists... "I must take it up with Bholu," she thought, "he is too lenient ... just because she is pretty and pleasant she gets away with anything ... what kind of woman is she ... her womb has not yet filled ... what have all the whisperings and giggles, the heaving and groaning night after night served…five years now and her womb is barren. If I ask her to observe a special 'vrat' she tosses her head and walks off…"

Basanti reflected on the Suchi who first stepped into their house after marriage… she would never concede a point in any discussion, but she was soft and pliant … she observed 'vrats' that Basanti recommended … she even allowed Basanti to tie a 'taveez' round her wrist with the hope that she would get pregnant. Everything was fine till Suchi went for the two year management course to Bangalore. Something happened … the soft and pliant daughter-in-law had transformed into a sharp tongued, terse voiced woman who did not care about what anybody in the family felt. It was as if some magic spell had been cast on her… Basanti suddenly perked up … that was it… magic would counteract that effect. She had to do something otherwise she would lose control… 'look at Bholu," she thought, "he will give up anything for the crisp freshly fried fish and he is just going off drinking a glass of milk because it is getting late for his wife? I must not waste any time, I must call Sukhram…" She scribbled a few lines on a postcard and sent Rama to post it. In a few days, Sukhram the family tantrik landed up. He knew the family well and made his entry into the house only after he was sure all members except Basanti would be away. Once he arrived, Basanti sent Rama also off on an errand so that she and Sukhram could conduct their business in confidence. Clad in a saffron dhoti with a brown Kashmiri shawl covering his torso, Sukhram was a tall, broad shouldered man with sharp intuitive eyes and a surprisingly gentle voice. "So Basantiji, what is the problem, you look troubled…" he asked. "Baba, it is Bholu I'm worried about …he is well, but he talks less and less with me these days…" Basanti began, tentatively, tremulously… Sukhram guffawed and replied,

"Bholu's mother, he is way past the suckling days... now he has other needs, which you can't satisfy, so he will naturally be under the spell of the woman who satisfies his needs. That is the way of life... you surely know it."

Looking at one spot on the floor, Basanti said, in a dangerously quiet voice, "that isn't all... my daughter-in-law has started openly criticizing me and my actions and Bholu smilingly hears her out ... he doesn't even contradict her, leave alone reprimanding... he does exactly what she wants him to do ... I can't allow that, Baba... it is as if she has worked some magic on him... as for her... after studying outside for two years she has become completely carefree and boldly questions me... and he allows her to... no, no... Baba, we must put a stop to this before things go out of hand... we must get a nice docile 'bahu' for my Bholu... that is why I called you..."

"Aaahaaan, Bholu ki maa, this puts everything in a completely different light... it is a very serious matter... let me think ... what can we do?"

He sat erect and closed his eyes, lost in deep thought... he was wondering how much he should fleece this old woman for... of course he should not be greedy and quote an unreasonably high amount. After all, he thought, it was her mother-in-law who had generously fed him so often in the past... in fact but for that old lady's kindness he would have been out on the streets... Basanti had been a good daughter-in-law, she had retained him as the power to whom the whole family turned when something was beyond human capacity. Though her sons were all grown up, married and financially independent, she reigned as the head of the family, no leaf turned without her nod!

Basanti sat quietly, discreetly slipping a betel leaf and nut into her mouth.

"Hmmm… Bholu ki Maa…" he whispered, bending forward, "there is only one way out for us…"

"Han…han…" she whispered, "we are forced into it… tell me…"

Sukhram pursed his lips and said, "You have to be very careful, tactful and patient… it will take time but it will surely work…"

Basanti gave a twisted smile and said, "Do you doubt my capabilities? Ok, tell me, we don't have much time, soon my old man will return from the Mutt and he must not see you here at any cost…he may be old and deaf but his mind is sharp as ever…"

"Yes…yes…Bholu ki Maa… we will have to resort to a lethal weapon… I use it very rarely… and…"

He scratched his hairy chest hesitantly and examining his fingernails he started studiously cleaning the grime off with his left thumbnail.

"Yes… tell me how much and I will arrange for it…have I ever failed you before?"

"Mmmm… I will need two thousand five hundred rupees, you pay me one thousand now and you can pay the rest when it is convenient for you…"

Basanti heaved herself up, waddled off to her room and bent to open her secret metal trunk. Taking out the handkerchief bundle, she carefully unwrapped it and peeled off ten hundred rupee notes from the roll of money. Rolling up the notes into her waist, she wrapped the rest of the money back in the kerchief and placed it back in the trunk. Closing the trunk she pushed it under the cot and went to give the money to Sukhram. She felt a pang of guilt when she remembered that she was actually instructed by Bholu to give the money to her sister Rani. Comforting herself that she would soon replace it, Basanti slid down onto her haunches against the wall and watched Sukhram mould a lump of clay deftly into the shape of a woman with his hands. He drew lines and curves on the clay figure with his thumbnail, muttering some 'mantra' under his breath. Once he finished, he took a speck of 'sindoor' from a conch shell and smearing it on the clay figure, he wrapped the figure in a banyan leaf. He then secured the wrapping with a piece of red string and held it out to Basanti. She took it and gently tied it to her sari end, waiting for his instructions.

"First of all," he said, "keep the figure out of sight. Then, talk with Bholu about how upset you are with your 'bahu's' behavior. Gently provoke him by pointing out that no 'bahu' is allowed to stay on in our culture if she fails to bear a child… that it is your kindness that she is not only allowed to stay but also treated well… that barrenness is not something our society takes kindly… talk with him so that she overhears you… it will be a warning for her. Then wait for the time when she next becomes unclean… on the fourth day, carefully halve a lime, place the clay figure between the halves, pierce the needle I have given you through it… wrap the lump in this white cloth and throw it into the trash can in the dead of night. By the morning she will have succumbed to a sudden attack of severe fits."

Basanti gave him the money wordlessly and nodded silently. He took the money and deftly secured it into the folds of his loincloth. She went down on her knees and touched her forehead to his feet. He blessed her and quickly walked off without a backward glance. Walking back, Basanti pulled Suchi's handkerchief off the clothesline and wrapped her bundle into it. She placed it in her trunk and went about her work with a satisfied smile. Gathering the clean clothes from the clothesline in the verandah, she saw her husband walking in from his outing. She heaved a sigh of relief that her business with Sukhram finished before her husband's return. As he went into the bathroom to wash his feet, she set on the table his lunch of rice, dal, four pieces of fried brinjal, two pieces of ripe tomato, a pinch of salt and a green chilli. She liberally doused his rice with ghee. Noticing this, her husband gave his toothless grin and slyly asked what the reason for her good mood was. She wordlessly stood while he finished his meal and then sat down on the low stool in the kitchen to have her own lunch. After doling out Rama's lunch onto his plate, she went into the bedroom to stretch her back for a brief rest.

Bholu and Suchi returned together in the evening. Basanti was particularly solicitous to her 'bahu' and had got everything ready for Rama to fry vegetable cutlets for the evening snack. "Mmmm… what is it, Ma… you seem to be in a very good mood…" Bholu asked, while Suchi simply smiled to herself and walked into their room.

Later in the evening they all sat together in front of the T.V., eating their evening snacks. Once the English news was over, Suchi went back into the room to rest a while. Basanti, seized the opportunity and sidling up to Bholu, asked him, "What happened, my son, you went off without eating this morning, are you unwell… or angry?"

Not taking his eyes off the TV screen he said that it was nothing at all, just that it was getting late for Suchi. Smoothing the piece of cloth she was darning, she smilingly retorted that she had never ever seen him letting pass a plate of rice and fried fish before. Not getting any attention from Bholu she angrily muttered, "How is the 'bahu's' work so important suddenly that you don't even eat … and she … you see how rude she is to me… you don't even reproach her for using that tone with me… what has come over you… what kind of day am I seeing… my own flesh and blood ignoring the way in which I am treated… it hurts…" Basanti let flow the copious tears that she had bottled up since the morning. "Ma… please stop this fuss… Suchi was not really insulting you … in fact there was some truth in what she said this morning… now please leave so that I can watch the game in peace…"

Basanti walked off thoughtfully and wondered what had come over her son. Soon she would put an end to all this nonsense, she thought to herself as she settled down to read the Oriya magazine. Two weeks passed with Basanti keeping a watch on Suchi's movements at home, silently biding her time. One fine evening while they were watching TV, Bholu suddenly said, "Oh, Ma… don't have any prawn or fish cooked for me in the mornings… Suchi needs to leave early and I will be dropping her off … I don't want her travelling by rickshaw … and I don't have time to return for lunch … so…" Basanti almost fell off her seat. "Bahu has to go to office early so you will stop eating fish on weekdays… what is this world coming to these days… or is it only MY son who is behaving so strangely…? He brings home a 'bahu' of his choice, yes, she is pretty, and clever… but what is the reason for you to become so unreasonable? She doesn't bother about our customs… she is too modern… but what use is her being able to drive a car and earn an income of 3000 rupees per month if she cannot bear the fruit of your marriage… it is five years now… she is as barren as a desert… we have been kind enough to keep her in the family… would anyone else keep such a bahu?" Hearing this tirade, Suchi went white and Bholu led her away to their room. Thereafter Suchi stayed away from Basanti and so did Bholu. They did not sit together in the evenings anymore. Basanti relentlessly waited for Suchi's periods to start so she could carry out the plot. The impudent hussy, she would learn a lesson soon… turning Bholu against her. She was confident that her plot would be effective and did not mind Bholu's terse attitude to her. Suchi always got her periods with regularity and Basanti had kept count of the days. Assuming that the girl must have got her periods as usual, on the fourth day, Basanti sliced a lime in two, wedged the clay figure between the slices, tied the string round it and wrapping it in the cloth she threw it into the dustbin outside the gate. It was midnight and Basanti quietly walked back into the house.

The next morning Bholu got up early, washed his face and sat at the dining table, quietly lost in thought. "Arrey, Bholu... what has come over you... no bed tea and you've woken up... what is the matter... are you well?" Basanti laughed and touched the back of her palm to his forehead.

"Yes, Maa... I'm fine... I have to talk with you ... I don't know how you're going to react... first the good news is that Suchi is pregnant... we got it confirmed... and I am so happy... she will give up her job ... and given the fact that you don't take too kindly to her these days ... there is no point in both of you staying in the same house... it would be good for you to shift to Bhai's house for about a year. Her family would also be visiting her. Besides I don't want her to have any stress... Maa... what's happening... are you OK?"

"Nothing my son... just feeling faint... 'Beta'... that five thousand rupees you had given me to keep for your aunt... I took out 1000 and put in the Lingaraj temple 'hundi.'

Oh, Maa... is that all...as if I would mind your giving money to the temple... maybe it is the blessings of Lingaraj that your bahu's womb is filled... I'm so happy that you don't mind shifting to Bhai's house"

Basanti silently nodded and looked at the sparrows perched on the clothesline, pecking at each other... "If he is happy I am too...," she thought...

Till Death Do Us Part...

One more day has passed, ruminates Urvashi, stacking up the old newspapers alongside the storeroom shelf...what have I done and what am I going to do...it does not matter. It is a life of stacking – dirty linen, freshly washed linen, used dishes, to be used dishes, old newspapers. The lethargy is killing but does not really kill.

She is rooted, almost frozen in time. What do I want from life, she wonders...I have a devoted husband in Guru. He is the epitome of perfection. So clean, fresh, punctual, courteous, concerned. A successful bureaucrat, a dutiful son, an amiable person, never known to fly off the handle, so predictable. That was it, Urvashi realized, so totally predictable that she was forced to rein in her spontaneity. Before marriage, every day was a glorious adventure.

She never knew what she was going to eat till their Amma or Paati lifted the lids off the dishes at meal times. The pleasure of seeing something they liked filled the room with shouts and squeals of delight, Usha recalled. The gleaming expectation in all their eyes and the barely controlled dribble of expectant saliva from the corner of their lips as she, her sister Arati and brothers Anit and Punit gathered around the dining table Urvashi often thought, would have made a suitable picture to paint for Van Gogh!

Guru was the antithesis of her personality and his family prided that opposites attract, so their marriage would be perfect. Guru, Urvashi discovered, did not like surprises and right from clothes to bed / bath linen, color combinations were matched and set. Once he got married Guru expected that his wife would adapt to the style. Insofar as food and eating were concerned, there was a fixed menu for every meal, every day of the week.

When they moved out from the family home after three years and set up their own home Urvashi ventured to try and dish out 'idli' instead of the stipulated 'puri' for breakfast and was met with a surprised growl, 'What happened, have we run out of wheat flour or have I got the day of the week wrong?' No appreciation of the fluffy white melt in the mouth 'idlis' or the five varieties of chutney to go alongwith them or the artistic plating she had struggled to perfect. 'You must know by now that any change from the routine puts me out and I can't afford to be out of sorts in the first hour of my working day, Urvashi…' 'Sorry,' Urvashi said and moved away. He gulped his tea, snatched his briefcase and walked out.

Urvashi was too tired and put off by Guru's reaction to even taste the breakfast. Just as she was putting it away, she heard a boisterous voice at the entrance… 'Aha, Bhabhi, I'm just in time…' Turning around she found Punpun, the younger brother of Guru's long time friend standing with an expectant grin.

Without waiting for an invitation, he walked in, pulled out a chair and sat at the dining table. Usha smilingly laid a place for him. 'This stuff looks too good to be eaten…Bhabhi, you must teach me the art of plating. When I get married, I can at least do that!' Having given due attention to the plating, Punpun helped himself to the idlis while Urvashi served out the various chutneys into the small, delicately engraved bowls at the side. She smilingly watched while he started eating. At least there was someone who appreciated her efforts! Having satiated himself, Punpun rose, lightly rubbing his stomach and remarked, 'I don't think Gurubhai deserves you…you're too good for him.'

Urvashi laughingly rebuked him for overstepping his limits and led him out into the smokers' corner as he pushed back his chair with a satisfied grunt. While he lit his cigarette, he gazed at her through narrowed lids. She began to feel a bit uncomfortable and left saying she had some unfinished chore. In the kitchen she went about clearing the breakfast dishes for the maid to wash later on.

She undid her apron and turning to hang it on the doorknob, she found Punpun standing uncomfortably close. He led her gently to the couch in the living room and she did not protest. Without a word they made love and she found her body awakening in a way she had never imagined. He got up after a while and with a gentle kiss on the nape of her neck he left.

Urvashi lay on the couch wondering what had come over her. Strangely she did not feel guilty or upset. She got up a while later, and went about her work. She found her own lack of shock and dismay at what she had done, rather strange but not unsettling. It was body responding to body and nothing more… but was it really so simple? She felt no love or attraction for Punpun but what happened between them was real, her sudden desire was real and she had not fantasized about someone else when her body responded to his.

When Guru returned from work he brought her a bunch of flowers for having been short tempered at breakfast. She smilingly placed the flowers in a vase and watched him as he took his tea into the smokers' corner. He was full of good humor all through dinner and they closed the day with a game of chess. He reached out to her in bed and she gave herself to him.

Lying beside him afterwards she wondered at herself. Who am I and what do I want... it was also not as if she had wanted to make love to Punpun. Whatever made her behave the way she did... she was not unhappy or regretful about her life or choices. When she looks back at her life there were certainly nfinite possibilities, but she had made her choices. Having done so, she made her adjustments and was quite content to do so. There were the odd days of friction but on the whole hers was a life following a steady course.

She needed to understand that life is like that... unpredictable at times. She needed to understand that along with our experiences, our perspective also keeps changing; what is right or wrong is not permanent or indelible. She needed to understand that what was true of her today will not be so tomorrow. She turned to her side and tried to sleep. 'I should tell Guru...' she thought. She would do it in the morning.

The next morning she got busy tidying up Guru's briefcase before getting his bed tea ready. Her hand chanced upon a packet of condoms. Strange, she thought since they did not practice birth control. Just then Guru woke up and taking in the scene, almost exploded in anger...suddenly changed his mind and said that he was tired of keeping up a façade. She wordlessly shut the briefcase and sat on a stool, waiting. Guru got up and restlessly lit a cigarette ignoring the ban on smoking inside the house. He spoke about his affair with his secretary which had been going on since five years. Geraldine was not allowing him to end the affair, he said...she threatened to kill herself every time he wanted to break off. She forced him to keep the affair going.

Urvashi slowly started understanding her husband. His mania for perfection, his routines were a way of trying to clean the dirt of his deceit away; no, worse, they camouflaged any cause for suspicion. The family would be at sixes and sevens ensuring routines were maintained and be blind to any strange behavior from his side. Urvashi recalled his behavior the previous morning when she had changed the breakfast menu. The disturbance and stress his behavior had caused, filled her mind with a blind rage. 'How dare he....' she fumed. She pulled her towel from the clothes rack and marched off for her shower. The deceit which Guru had been carrying on for so many years baffled and angered her. What should she do?

Coming out of the shower, Urvashi dressed slowly thinking all the time. She could see that Geraldine mattered for Guru emotionally and physically. There was no way that was going to die down and his marriage to her was because he did not have the courage to take a stand and marry a woman who was not a Hindu. Urvashi asked him why he had not told his parents about Geraldine. 'I did,' Guru said, 'but they threatened to kill themselves if I tried to marry Geraldine.

Urvashi did not know how to react. His parents knowingly deceived her family. They surely must have known about his continuing relationship with Geraldine even after marriage and colluded in hiding the truth from her.

Urvashi realized the fragility of her situation. She was a stranger to the city. Any display of anger, emotional breakdown on her part would be labelled by Guru and his family as mental imbalance needing medical attention. She had heard of many cases and was determined not to let such a fate befall her.

She dressed calmly, with Guru watching her cautiously. She completed her puja and went into the kitchen. It was Tuesday - 'idli' day and she carefully poured out the smooth batter into their cups and set them for steaming.

'Geraldine...' a voice screamed inside her head...'so religiously observing vegetarian and non vegetarian days week after week...chanting the ***ashtalakshmi sloka*** every Friday, visiting the Shiva temple every Monday... he carries on an affair with a Geraldine...' Urvashi goes breathless with rage. Steadying her shaking hands she spoons out the 'idlis' from their cups. Releasing them carefully into a dish she clears away the steam coated bowls into the sink. The steam singes her fingers and she runs the tap allowing the water to cool her fingers. She finds a strange sense of coolness in her head also and wryly wonders if it would have made any difference if it was a Reena or Meena her husband was having an affair with.

Urvashi tries desperately to gauge what exactly outrages and upsets her. Is it Guru's extramarital affair, is it his hypocrisy, is it his duplicity, is it the ease with which both he and his family conned her and her family into the marriage... she finds no clear answer.

Sitting across while Guru has breakfast she asks how he would react if she had to tell him a similar story about herself. He looks up and says he would kill her...

Smiling wryly at the hypocrisy Urvashi rises and helps him to some more idlis and chutney. Moving into the kitchen she quietly pulls out the gas cylinder. She removes the saucepan of milk from the stove and turns on the flame full force. Striking a match she releases the valve of the cylinder.

The force of the explosion of the throws Guru out against the living room sofa...

Meeting Ground

Lakshmi stood in front of the blue framed full length mirror in her sister's house, looking at her reflection. The chiffon sari draped quite well but she was not happy. Pulling the sari pleats into place she peered at the face staring back at her from the mirror. 'Are my cheeks bloated... nooo... then why does my body feel awkward and movements seem ungainly?'

She sighed impatiently, sank into her chair and went back to the newspaper editorial she was reading... there was nobody at home. Her mother had gone off to help her cousin with the spice stall he had recently set up in the supermarket; her sister was away at work and her nephew and niece would return from college only after another three hours. The sounds from the kitchen floated up as Bhadramma set about washing and drying the breakfast dishes.

A week ago Lakshmi would also have been away at work in her airline ticketing office. She restlessly jumped up and sat on the edge of the bed before stretching herself out, helplessly. Lying flat on her back she gazed up at the ceiling. It was such luxury to have a whole day at her disposal...not one but as many as she wished for as long as she wanted. There was no need to jump out of bed and hurry around getting ready to catch the 8.30 bus in the morning... no pressure of mentally listing out the sales calls she had to make in the day... the acid rush into her mouth at the thought of how to deal with the questions fielded by her boss during the daily review session had become a thing of the past. Aahhh... she deserved this break. She turned to her side and opened the newspaper lying limp in her hand. There was a restlessness, something bothering her.

No... things were not alright. Lakshmi sat bolt upright and her thoughts went back to the conversation of the previous evening. She did a re-run of the scene. When she had greeted her sister, laughing, 'Guess what - my nephew, that is, your son, has been selected for the regional football match...isn't it great... he is so excited... I can't wait to shop for him... we have to get him new shoes, T shirts, sleeping bag...' Her sister seemed not to have heard her at all... 'Akka, I'm talking to you...' Her sister just continued ridding herself of her handbag and other work paraphernalia. Lakshmi sensed something was amiss. 'Akka, what is the matter... are you feeling ill... a headache...' Her sister impatiently asked that she be left alone.

'Amma, guess what...' her son Rahul came bounding into the room, eyes and lips smiling with pleasure. 'Yes, I know..., your aunt has already told me and also drawn plans to take you shopping... so spare me the details...' Rahul looked across at his aunt questioningly. Lakshmi was puzzled at her sister's abrupt reaction to Rahul, the son she doted on. She left the room perturbed...

Why does Akka have these sudden mood swings, Lakshmi wondered gazing out of the window. Of late it was becoming too frequent and particularly surfaced when Lakshmi spoke with her. 'I must get to the bottom of this...' Lakshmi thought and waited for her mother to return for lunch.

While lying beside her mother after lunch Lakshmi spoke about the problem. 'Akka gets into a temper so quickly these days, Amma..' she said. 'The temper seems to be sparked off by me in some way, Amma...' She then narrated the previous day's incident. Her mother sighed and said 'It was a mistake for you to give up your job, Lakshmi.'

'What has that got to do with Akka becoming short tempered,' Lakshmi countered. 'I don't depend on any of you to entertain me…'

'You don't need anyone to entertain you, Lakshmi, but a change in your life causes ripples in other people's lives… surely you can see that? Your sister has generously made room for both of us in her family. We should always be grateful for that and remember our place.

Please think of everything as a whole, not only your job and your time. If only you had continued to have a 9 – 5 job you would have a fixed schedule. Things would have gone on smoothly… out of the blue you talk about taking a break and just give up your job. True, you have worked like a donkey for five years… but you had a pattern, a schedule, a routine, like everyone else in the house… and the goings on the house, the family, also had a pattern, a sequence… your stay at home status has disturbed that…'

Lakshmi returned to her room lost in thought. Amma was so right. Family and hierarchy, were two aspects she had completely ignored. She had forgotten that she had been taken in by a family, her sister's family and cared for by it. *She* was not family but was generously considered part of the family. As long as she had a 9 – 5 job which kept her out of the house from 8 a.m. to 6 p.m. everything was fine. But with her new state of freedom she was unconsciously treading on the family's toes. How could she forget the generosity of her sister?

'I should not disturb her life,' Lakshmi thought. She went to the cellar and pulled out the newspaper of the previous Sunday. Turning the pages she folded out the 'Matrimonials' column. Scanning through, she found a notice… '50 year old divorcee, living in U.K., looking for female companion in mid

30s. Slim, fair, beautiful woman with a sense of humour can correspond to Post Box No 358. Lakshmi furtively looked around and taking out her diary, copied the address... this would be the best way out ... she thought...

Dosa and Dhansak...

The dawn of Sunday brought an indescribable exhilaration in Ratan's heart. It was the day when Amma prepared a special breakfast. White, soft dosa touched lightly with home made butter, accompanied by spicy coconut chutney. Amma had been at the grindstone late Saturday night, whipping up a light batter of the rice and dal mixture which she had soaked immediately after lunch. The rhythmic sound of the grinder had lulled Ratan's whisky laden brain to sleep.

Twenty five year old Ratan was the second child in the Ramanuj Iyer family living off Kingsway. He was already an upper division clerk in Bright Bank and hoped to clear the officers' examinations in six months. A lean, fair, good looking bloke, he was mostly wrapped in thoughts of himself, with an amused smile always playing on his lips and a lazy repartee for almost any occasion. His mother was on the look out for a suitable bride for him. He was neither keen nor disinclined... he was ambivalent to most things in life. He did not believe in burdening people with any high Ideology or opinions...live and let live...he said.

His job was ideal for his nature requiring nothing more than routine steps in writing fixed deposit receipts, slipping them into plastic covers and stacking in the delivery tray... either to be delivered immediately to the client or kept in safe custody on behalf of the client.

'Excuse me, can you tell me where I can find the Personnel Officer?' Ratan looked up to see who the soft, husky voice belonged to. Light brown eyes smiled down at him. He showed her the way and went back to his work. Later in the afternoon he found the same girl come to his side of the counter and introduce herself. 'Hi, I'm Yasmin,' joined as Probationary Officer today. I've been asked to learn counter work. Can I start with you?' He took in her wavy hair falling loosely around her shoulders, formal black, knee length skirt and white collared blouse, a black scarf loosely knotted around the neck.

He welcomed her and then went about explaining his work. She listened attentively and made notes in her little diary. He asked her to watch them at work in order to understand the basics. She sat for two whole days watching them at work. On the third day Ratan magnanimously allowed Yasmin to stack the completed fixed deposit receipts in serial order. At the end of one week he introduced her to writing the 'day book.'

There were not many female staff in the bank and in Ratan's branch the only other female staff was Devi, the woman who went around handing out drinking water twice a day; she had been absorbed into the work force on compassionate grounds following the untimely demise of her husband who had been a messenger boy. Yasmin was a whiff of fresh air to the otherwise staid and very male crowd. Everyone in the branch was taken in by her openness combined with a calm efficiency. She was different from them, but her distinction did not jar the senses. Every morning they would all eagerly wait for the wave of perfume that invaded their nostrils and her gay, light, morning greetings.

During the lunch break Yasmin sat alone in a small room adjacent to the large canteen which dished out hot meals and snacks for the men. She carried a packed lunch of sandwiches and a small thermos of milk. She ate while reading.

One afternoon Ratan walked across to her with his plate of lemon rice. 'Can I join you,' he asked and Yasmin, her mouth full of a sandwich bite, gestured for him to do so. He placed his plate and glass of buttermilk on the table and hauled himself a chair from the canteen. He offered his lemon rice for Yasmin to taste and she offered him a sandwich. They concentrated on their food for the first five minutes and Yasmin then asked Ratan if he was a vegetarian. He laughed that he was born one but over time his favorite dish had become butter chicken with 'rumali roti!' Yasmin laughed that she would treat him to some of her special dishes sometime.

It became a pattern for Yasmin and Ratan to sit together for lunch everyday. On days that the work extended beyond 5 p.m. for Yasmin, Ratan also hung around and dropped her off near her home. One Saturday Yasmin asked Ratan to drop in for lunch on Sunday if he had nothing to better to do. 'I shall introduce you to a homely but exotic lunch,' she promised. Ratan accepted the invitation on the condition that she offer him some beer as well.

Ratan arrived at her house by 11.30 the next morning with a box of chocolates. Yasmin opened the door and led him in. The house was an old fashioned residential apartment with a large sprawling verandah, spacious rooms and bay windows. The windows and door were draped with thin muslin curtains and different kinds of music could be heard from different corners of the house. Yasmin's father, clad in a white pyjama and cotton vest greeted Ratan with a firm handshake and beckoned him to sit. Yasmin's brothers Minu and Naoshir came and shook hands with him. Yasmin's mother peeped out from behind the dining room curtain and nodded a greeting.

Guiding Ratan to a seat in the living room, Yasmin signaled her father to pour him a drink. Mr. Dadabhoy handed him a glass of beer and refilled his glass. Yasmin sat across with a glass of Fanta. Her father was an easy talker and entertained Ratan with interesting anecdotes in his office. Mrs. Dadabhoy came waddling in and helped herself to a glass of beer. Easing herself into a sofa, she sized Ratan up… 'have you eaten 'dhansak' before?' she asked. Ratan shook his head. 'Brahmin?' she asked. He nodded. 'I had better make some vegetarian dish as well… just in case…' she said and taking a huge, noisy gulp of beer she picked up her ladle and marched back to the kitchen.

The whole family sat for lunch as soon as Mrs. Dadabhoy called. The Sunday lunch, Ratan, observed, was just as eagerly awaited by Yasmin's family as the Sunday breakfast was in his home. The fragrance was delicious. Yasmin served Ratan some steaming hot flavoured rice and her mother passed him the tureen of 'dhansak.' The layers of lamb's meat resting on the bed of richly spiced dal looked attractive. Suddenly Ratan spotted the lumps of fat encircling the meat and gravy. His stomach turned and he gently pushed it away. Mrs. Dadabhoy quietly handed him a small dish of tomato gravy. He gratefully helped himself to some and started eating.

Chewing on her food noisily, Mrs. Dadabhoy looked at Ratan and Yasmin and said, 'Dosa and dhansak don't go together. It is better to be aware of facts early rather than suffer pain, my children…'

Printed in the United States
By Bookmasters